painting
your
favorite
BIRDS
STEP BY STEP

NANCY DALE KINNEY

NORTH LIGHT BOOKS

CINCINNATI, OHIO
www.artistsnetwork.com

Other fine North Light Books are available from your local bookstore, art supply store or direct from the publisher.

08 07 06 05 04   5 4 3 2 1

Library of Congress Cataloging-in-Publication Data

Kinney, Nancy Dale
    Painting your favorite birds step by step / Nancy Dale Kinney.
      p. cm.
    Includes index.
    ISBN 1-58180-512-8 (pbk. : alk. paper)
    1. Birds in art. 2. Acrylic painting--Technique. I. Title

ND2280.K56 2004
758'.3--dc22

Editor: Holly Davis
Designer: Mary Barnes Clark
Layout Artist: Jennifer Dailey
Production Coordinator: Kristen Heller
Photographer: Christine Polomsky

Metric Conversion Chart

to convert	to	multiply by
Inches	Centimeters	2.54
Centimeters	Inches	0.4
Feet	Centimeters	30.5
Centimeters	Feet	0.03
Yards	Meters	0.9
Meters	Yards	1.1
Sq. Inches	Sq. Centimeters	6.45
Sq. Centimeters	Sq. Inches	0.16
Sq. Feet	Sq. Meters	0.09
Sq. Meters	Sq. Feet	10.8
Sq. Yards	Sq. Meters	0.8
Sq. Meters	Sq. Yards	1.2
Pounds	Kilograms	0.45
Kilograms	Pounds	2.2
Ounces	Grams	28.4
Grams	Ounces	0.04

ABOUT THE AUTHOR

Nancy Dale Kinney has taught painting for 25 years. She is a familiar and popular instructor at seminars and at conventions such as the Society of Decorative Painters (SDP) Conference, Heart of Ohio Tole (HOOT), The Creative Painting Convention (CPC) and New England Tole (NET). Besides international travel teaching, she has instructed 100 women a week at her local community college. On top of this, she maintains a wholesale and retail business, Nancy Kinney's Paintin' House, with her husband, Doug. She has created over 150 painting packets and 8 books, 6 of which are about painting birds.

Nancy and her husband live in Hickory, North Carolina, located in the foothills of the Blue Ridge Mountains.

To learn more about Nancy Kinney's seminar teaching schedule, pattern packets or painting materials, use the following contact information:

Nancy Kinney's Paintin' House
421 14th Avenue NW
Hickory, North Carolina 28601

Phone: 828-327-2478
E-mail: kinney@twave.net
Web site: www.PictureTrail.com/nancykinney

Dedication

To God, my teacher,

and to Doug, my husband and best supporter.

ACKNOWLEDGMENTS

I feel blessed that God has allowed me the possibility to communicate to you some of my favorite beginner bird projects. I never dreamed my talents would develop into such wonderful and exciting opportunities.

I also thank my husband, Doug, who continues to love and support me in all of my new endeavors.

I will always be grateful to my acquisitions editor, Kathy Kipp, for developing with me the concept of writing a beginner bird-painting book. With her encouragement and trust, my dream has come true.

I would also like to express special appreciation to my editor, Holly Davis, for her patience and sincere caring as she helped me each step of the way. She was there with encouragement and honesty as we worked to bring this book to life.

My thanks also to my photographer, Christine Polomsky, who was so patient and good to work with as she guided me through the photoshoot.

TABLE OF CONTENTS

chapter one

*M*aterials

PAINT

All projects in this book are painted with Americana DecoArt Acrylics. Besides straight bottle colors, each project uses a mix called Animal Black. This is a color I developed specifically for painting realistic birds and other animals. You can order Animal Black, already mixed and bottled, directly from me (see Resources, page 126) or you can mix it yourself. To do this, pour out a puddle of Burnt Umber and a puddle of Lamp Black. With a palette knife, mix two parts of Burnt Umber with one part of Lamp Black.

In addition to Animal Black, you will use either Mix 1 or Mix 2 or both for almost every bird in this book. Both start with Animal Black. You would then pour a puddle of Light Buttermilk. Use your palette knife to mix the colors, and always carry the darker color to the lighter color. Mix 1 (medium gray) has less Light Buttermilk than Mix 2 (light gray).

Formulas for Animal Black, Mix 1 and Mix 2 are listed below. The paint names tell you which colors are in the mix. The numbers tell you the proportions, or how many parts of each color to use. The proportions are listed in the same order as the colors.

Lamp Black

Burnt Umber

Animal Black

Mix 2

Formulas for Most-Used Mixes

Animal Black: Burnt Umber + Lamp Black (2:1)

Mix 1: Light Buttermilk + Animal Black (2:1)

Mix 2: Light Buttermilk + Animal Black (3:1)

Mix 1

BRUSHES

With these ten brushes, you can paint every bird in this book!

Loew-Cornell

- 1-inch (25mm) wash, series 7550
  Used to paint background and large design areas.

- 2-inch (51mm) wash, series 7550
  Used to varnish finished project.

- flat chisel blenders (nos. 4, 6, 8, 12), series 7450
  These maintain an excellent chisel edge that's perfect for birds. In the projects they are simply referred to as flats.

- no. 1 liner, series 3350

Nancy Kinney

I developed the floral and dabber brushes for my uniquely simple painting technique, used throughout this book (see page 10). To order, see Resources on page 126.

- Nancy Kinney Floral Brush (one size) The synthetic filaments of this brush are soft with excellent spring action. They maintain a sharp chisel edge and provide extra control and coverage for stroking a flower petal or painting feathers or fur. Side- or double-loaded paint is easily blended on this brush.

- Nancy Kinney Dabber Brush (small, medium and large) In this book I use only the small dabber. This round simulated mongoose hair brush takes away the heartbreak of floating acrylic colors. Dab or pat dark and light values in the various areas of a design. Wipe the brush on a paper towel, and then blend the colors by dabbing or patting.

The last brush you'll need is a large old scruffy, about the size of a no. 12 flat, for applying gel retarder.

(bottom to top) Loew-Cornell 2-inch (51mm) wash, Loew-Cornell no. 12 flat chisel blender, Loew-Cornell no. 6 flat chisel blender, Loew-Cornell no. 1 liner, Nancy Kinney floral, Nancy Kinney small dabber.

Parts of the Brush

You'll find these brush parts referred to throughout this book. A little study now can save you from confusion as you paint.

corner of brush

flat surface

handle

side of brush

ferrule

chisel edge

SURFACES

Most projects in this book are painted on acid-free mounting board. Two projects in this book are painted on wooden plates. Of course, you can paint any bird on any paintable surface you choose.

Acid-free mounting board doesn't require any preparation for painting, but wood surfaces should be sanded and sealed. Use fine-grade sandpaper and wipe off the dust with a damp cloth. Apply water-based wood sealer with a large sponge brush. When the sealer is dry, sand lightly and wipe off the dust. This gives you a smooth painting surface.

OTHER MATERIALS

These items will round out your painting supplies:

• **Tracing paper** For tracing a pattern in preparation of transferring it to your painting surface.

• **White and gray transfer paper** A coated paper that's slipped, coating down, between the traced pattern and the painting surface. Used to transfer the pattern lines with a pen or stylus.

• **Ball point pen or stylus** For transferring patterns. See above.

• **Brush basin** Holds water for painting.

• **2- to 4-inch (51mm to 102mm) sponge roller** For rolling background colors on your painting surface.

• **Masterson's Sta-Wet Painter's Pal Palette** Used to hold and mix colors. This particular palette keeps the paint wet and can be covered between painting sessions.

• **Palette knife** For mixing paints.

• **Jo Sonja's Gel Retarder** Dampens the painting area for applying different color values. Aids in blending.

• **Plastic containers** Different sizes for holding gel retarder or varnish.

OTHER MATERIALS, continued

- **Paper towels** For wiping the brush and for giving rouged color to backgrounds.

- **Sea sponge** Used to create a marbled effect when applying background color.

- **Spray mist water bottle** Used to dampen the painting surface before applying sea sponged background color.

- **Plastic wrap** Used to create a marbled background effect.

- **Smoked-surface supplies** With a metal tablespoon, candle, candleholder and Krylon Matte Finish spray 1311, you can create a smoked background surface. The Krylon spray is a fixative.

- **Hair dryer** For drying paint quickly.

- **J.W. etc.'s Right-Step Water Base Clear Varnish** Gives the finished painting a protective covering and brings out the paint's luster. Matte, satin, semi-gloss and gloss finishes are available. I prefer satin.

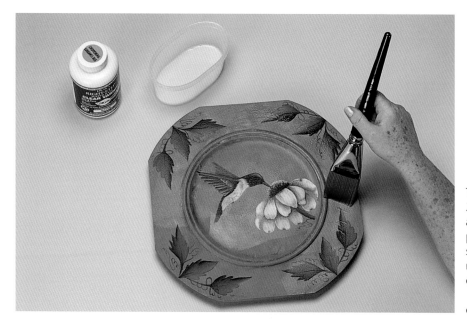

To varnish a finished project, dampen a 2-inch (51mm) wash brush with water and blot the excess moisture with a paper towel. Apply varnish in long strokes going one direction. Let dry and repeat varnishing in the opposite direction.

Varnishes differ, so read the bottle directions and adjust accordingly.

A WORD ABOUT MATS

Chances are you'll want to frame your bird paintings for display. When you do, consider using a framing mat. The effect can be striking. In fact, you should never give up on a painting until you've at least matted it. You'll notice that the first photo for most of the bird projects is matted. Compare that photo to the last one for the same project and you'll get an idea what matting can do.

The best way to select a mat (and a frame, for that matter) is to take your finished painting to a frame store, art supply store or hobby shop and experiment. Try mats of different colors. Compare mats with different shaped openings, like ovals or rectangles. I've designed a mat with a birdhouse-shaped opening, which you can order on my Web site (see Resources, page 126).

You put a lot of effort into your painting. Give it the finishing touches it deserves.

chapter two

Techniques

My painting technique can be described in three stages. At each stage, the individual body parts of birds must be painted in the direction of feather growth. This direction, generally toward the tail, is indicated on my patterns with tiny lines. Chiseling (see sidebar) creates the appearance of feathers blending into each other. Chiseling may be necessary at all three stages of painting.

The first stage is basecoating. This is done with two or three coats to assure opaque coverage. I find it's easier to paint up to the pattern lines without actually touching and, consequently, losing them. Basecoating is mostly done with a flat, but a liner may be used for small areas.

When the basecoating is complete and dry, you're ready to move on to the second stage. This consists of adding dark values. Use an old scruffy brush to apply gel retarder to the area you intend to paint next. The retarder dampens the surface, making blending easier. Practice will enable you to get the feel of how much gel to use. If you apply too much or the gel is runny, blot the area with a clean paper towel.

On my patterns I sometimes use crosshatching to indicate dark-value areas, although, to avoid making the pattern too busy, I do little of this on the birds.

To add a dark value, pick up a small amount of color on a dabber brush and dab in the color. Wipe the brush on a paper towel and blend where the dark value meets the basecoat color (medium value). To blend, dab gently to softly merge the two values.

When the second stage is complete and dry, you're ready for the third stage—adding light values, highlights and accents. I mark these areas on my patterns with dots unless I think the dots make the pattern too busy, as is often the case with birds.

Again, use your scruffy brush to apply gel retarder on the area you intend to paint. Dab in your color with the brush recommended in the project directions, wipe the brush and blend.

When your painting is "finished," place it in an area of your home where you relax. Study your design, coming back to it over a day or two. Can you see the dark and light values, or does the painting seem dull? Reinforce your values until they seem right, following the same technique you originally used to lay them. Once you're happy with your painting, varnish it and, if appropriate, mat and frame it.

Chiseling

1 To show the feathers blending into each other at different colors or body parts, work the paint with the chisel edge of the brush. This is called chiseling or chiseling in. Here you see that I've chiseled the edge of a gray breast where it would meet the neck.

2 Here I'm chiseling a black neckband back into the gray breast.

PARTS OF THE BIRD

This diagram will help you identify the parts of the bird referred to in the project instructions.

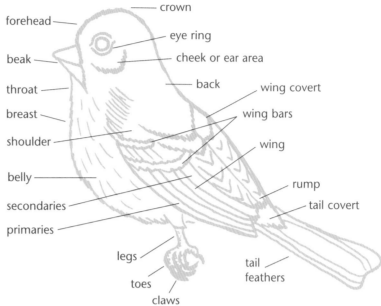

crown

forehead

eye ring

beak

cheek or ear area

back

throat

wing covert

breast

wing bars

shoulder

wing

belly

rump

secondaries

tail covert

primaries

legs

tail feathers

toes

claws

PAINTING ORDER

When painting birds, the body parts that lie under others are done first. This is especially apparent at the basecoating stage, which is generally done in this order:

1. tail
2. beak
3. back, rump and tail covert
4. wings
5. wing coverts and neck
6. head
7. belly, breast
8. eye and eye-ring
9. legs, toes and claws

After the bird is basecoated, you'll add things like feather separations, wing bars, dark values and light values.

8th

6th

2nd

5th

7th

4th

3rd

9th

1st

Loads

Side Load

1 Place your paint puddle on a clear space on the palette. Dampen your brush in water and blot it on a paper towel. Pull your brush forward so one side goes through the paint.

2 Bring your brush back up through the paint so both brush surfaces are loaded on the same side.

3 Compare this side-loaded brush to the corner-loaded brush in step 2 below.

4 Pull a stroke on your palette or paper towel to remove excess paint and to blend the color into the brush. Then pull a stroke on your painting surface. This is a stroke made from a side-loaded brush.

Corner Load

1 Dip just the corner of your brush in the paint. Blend once on the palette before beginning to paint your surface.

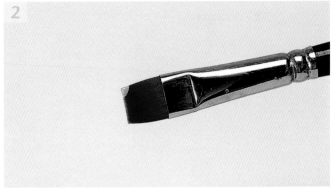

2 This is the corner-loaded brush. Compare it to the side-loaded brush in step 3 above.

Double Load

1 This load uses two colors. Load one flat surface of your brush in the color of lighter value.

2 Turn the brush over and load the opposite surface in the same color.

3 Drag one side of the same brush surface through the darker value.

4 Turn the brush and side load the darker value on the same side of the opposite surface.

5 Pull a stroke on your palette to blend. You are now ready to paint your double-loaded stroke on your painting surface.

LOADS, continued

Flat Surface Double Load

1 Once you have your two paint puddles, drag out a bit of each color. Then drag one surface of your floral or flat brush through the lighter value. The brush is almost perpendicular to the paint.

2 Turn over the brush and drag the opposite flat surface through the darker value. See the next page for strokes created with the flat surface double load.

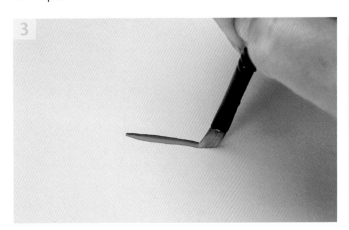

3 This smooth stroke is made using the chisel edge of a flat surface double-loaded brush.

4 This choppy stroke is also made with a flat surface double-loaded brush. To create the choppiness, move the brush to the right and left as you apply more pressure. This stroke is good for painting branches or certain types of feather indications.

C-Strokes and Curlicue

C-Strokes

C-strokes are usually clustered in groups like these to indicate wing covert feathers and wing feather edges. The elongated C-strokes on the right are made with a flat surface double-loaded brush. The short, cupped strokes on the left are actually a series of tiny C-strokes in a V shape, made with the chisel edge of a side-loaded floral brush.

Here an elongated C-stroke delineates the pupil of the eye. It was painted with a no. 1 liner flattened in Animal Black and side loaded with Light Buttermilk.

Curlicue

To create a curlicue, lightly thin your paint with water and pull your stroke with a liner. Curlicues are used for vines or branch details.

chapter three

*B*ackgrounds

BACKGROUND SURFACE TECHNIQUES

Basecoats

For even coverage, apply your basecoat with a 2- to 4-inch (51mm to 102mm) sponge roller. Dampen the roller in water and squeeze the excess moisture into a paper towel. Then load the roller with your basecoat color.

The basecoat must be opaque, which means you'll have to apply at least two coats, allowing the paint to dry in between. On the left you see the first layer of paint. On the right an extra layer has been applied, making the color opaque. Strive for a smooth, eggshell texture.

Rolled (multi-colored)

For variety, you can add a different color after your first coat of basing.

1 Basecoat your surface with two coats of paint, letting the first dry, but not the second.

3 Immediately roll the second color in. Here I've used Light Buttermilk. Rolling this second color in over wet paint gives you a whitewashed effect. Let dry.

2 While the second basecoat remains wet, squirt on your second color in a circular motion.

Blended Color

This surface technique gives your painting depth. It's also called "rouged color."

1 Basecoat your painting surface and let it dry. Using a 1-inch (25mm) or larger wash brush, dampen the surface with gel retarder in a slip-slap X motion. Blot the surface with a paper towel if the gel is too runny.

2 Now you may add touches of color to complement your painting. Begin with your lightest value. Wipe your brush often as you blend into the gel. If the surface begins to dry, stop, blow dry and redampen with gel before continuing. When you've finished applying the light value, let it dry.

3 Dampen your surface again with gel. Apply your darker value so it will show around your design and bring it forward. If you want to add further depth, let the paint dry, redampen with gel and repeat the darker color.

4 This is a completed blended-color surface.

Background Surface Techniques, continued

Smoked and Smoked Plus Rouged Color

1 Basecoat your painting surface as explained on page 16. Let it dry. Light the candle in the holder and let it burn a couple of minutes to get a good flame. Hold the scooped side of a metal tablespoon over the flame until you get a carbon build-up on the spoon and a steady stream of black smoke rising just above the spoon.

2 Hold your painted surface over the black stream of smoke, allowing the smoke to adhere to the surface. Continue smoking the surface until you have the desired darkness.

3 Here is a smoked plate.

4 Immediately spray your smoked surface with Krylon Matte Finish 1311, holding the can about 12 inches (30.5cm) from the surface. This keeps the smoke from smudging. At this point you may stop or you may add rouged color, as explained in the following steps.

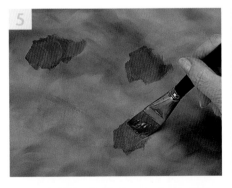

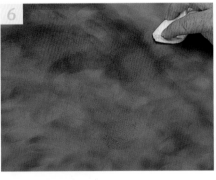

5 To add color, dampen a 1-inch (25mm) wash brush with gel retarder and wipe off the excess on a paper towel. Then slip-slap a color in the unsmoked areas.

6 Gently blend the color into the smoked surface with a soft paper towel.

7 This is the finished smoke-plus-rouged-color surface. You can add the color before you paint your bird, as I've done here, or after.

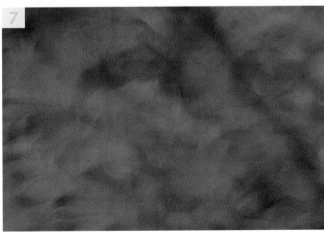

Sponge and Plastic Wrap (Marbleizing)

1 Basecoat your painting surface as explained on page 16. Let dry. Dampen a sea sponge with water and squeeze out the excess moisture, using a paper towel in your hand. Spray your surface with water.

2 Dip the sea sponge in the paint and then dab it on your palette to remove excess paint.

3 Dab the sponge onto your surface. The paint will bleed lightly into the water on the surface. Be sure not to completely cover the background.

4 Immediately lay plastic wrap over your sponged surface. Press down on the wrap with your hands, allowing the paint to work into the creases of the wrap. Then remove the plastic wrap.

5 Here is the completed sponge-and-plastic-wrap surface. The effect is sometimes called marbleizing, but you can see it also suggests branches and foliage.

Background Design Elements

The design elements on the next few pages are used in the project backgrounds. When you paint a bird, you may choose to use the same background design I did, or you may want to substitute something else.

Twiggy Branch

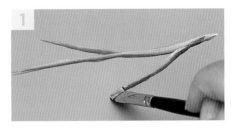

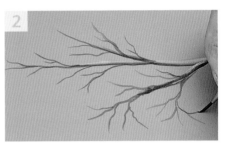

Important!

Colors used in the background design elements may change from project to project, but the technique remains the same. Don't be afraid to experiment with other color combinations. You may also choose to use different size brushes, depending on what works best for you and on the size you choose to make your painting.

1 Flat surface double load a no. 8 flat with Burnt Umber and Fawn. With the Fawn on top, paint a continuous curvy stroke for the main branch. Add a few secondary branches. You'll need to add pressure to the brush.

2 Using a no. 1 liner and Burnt Umber thinned with water, pull jerky lines away from the main or secondary branches for twigs. When you start the stroke, overlap the "mother" branch using a little pressure on the brush to create a smooth connection.

Birch Branch

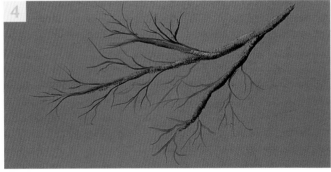

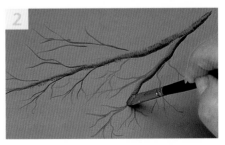

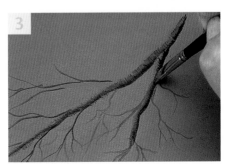

1 Basecoat the main branches with Fawn on the chisel edge of a no. 8 flat.

2 Pull out a few random twigs with Burnt Umber on a no. 1 liner. Let dry and then redampen with gel retarder. Flat surface double load the no. 8 flat with Animal Black (see page 6) and Fawn. Pull a stroke along the main branches with Fawn at the top of the brush.

3 To create the birch tree effect, pull the brush up in a series of short C-strokes along the branch. In this and the last photo, I've already completed these strokes on the main branch. Here I'm starting on the secondary branch.

4 While the branch is still wet, use the same no. 8 flat to lighten the upper part with curved C-strokes in Light Buttermilk.

Pine Branch

1 Several birds are painted with a pine branch. Although the colors vary, the technique remains the same. Using a slight pouncing motion with the chisel edge of a no. 8 flat, basecoat the branch in Asphaltum. Let dry.

2 Redampen the branch with gel retarder. Flat surface double load the no. 8 flat in Animal Black (see page 6) and Light Buttermilk and pounce along the branch with the Light Buttermilk on top of the brush. Let dry.

3 Redampen the branch with gel, expanding into the pine needle area. Using Black Green on a floral brush, pull needles from the branch outward. With the same brush and colors, you can also pull one or more secondary branches, as I have.

4 You may want to add Celery Green needles to lie on top of the darker needles.

Pinecone

1 Base the pinecone bud with two coats of Burnt Umber. Let dry

2 Dampen the cone with gel retarder. Using a no. 8 flat, darken the right side with Animal Black (see page 6) and lighten the left side with Burnt Sienna. Let dry.

3 Redampen the cone with retarder. Using just the tip of a floral brush, pull Burnt Sienna strokes from the bottom of the cone, staggering them up toward the stem. Let dry.

4 Redampen with retarder. Add a light value by pulling True Ochre strokes over the Burnt Sienna. Start on the left side of the cone and work to the right. The True Ochre will gradually lose strength, leaving the right side of the cone darker than the left. Let dry.

5 Redampen with gel and further lighten the left side of the cone with Moon Yellow.

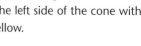

Leaf

1 Paint all green leaves with this technique. First base the leaf with a no. 8 flat and two coats of Antique Green for opaque coverage. Let dry.

2 Redampen with gel retarder. Using Black Green on a dabber, paint in the dark values. These are indicated on project patterns with crosshatching.

3 Wipe the excess paint from the brush and dab or lightly rub to blend. Let dry.

4 Redampen with gel retarder. Begin to lighten with Celery Green. Light-value areas are indicated on the project patterns with dots.

5 Wipe excess paint from the brush and dab or lightly rub to blend. Add Celery Green + Light Buttermilk to further lighten. Add a touch of accent value, which varies with your design. Sometimes the accent reflects a color from the bird or other design element in the painting.

Pussy Willows

1 Base the willow with a no. 8 flat and two coats of Light Buttermilk. Base the stem with two coats of Burnt Umber. Let dry.

2 Redampen the willow with gel retarder. Dab Mix 2 (see page 6) at the top of the stem with a dabber brush. Wipe the excess paint from the brush and dab up into the willow to blend.

3 While the willow remains damp, further darken with Black Green. Paint the left side of the stem with Animal Black (see page 6). Let dry.

4 Redampen with retarder. Add a touch of True Ochre just above the shadows. Add Light Buttermilk at the top to lighten.

Cherries

1 Using a no. 8 flat, basecoat the cherries with two or three coats of Deep Burgundy. Let dry between coats. Pull in the stem with Burnt Umber on a no. 1 liner, starting where the stem is attached to the limb.

2 Redampen the cherries with gel retarder. Using the dabber, shade with Black Plum where the cherries overlap, on the outside edge and in the throat. After shading a section, wipe the brush and dab to blend. Let dry.

3 Redampen the cherries with gel. Apply True Red using the dabber in front of the throat and down the left edges. You can further build the lights with True Red + Cadmium Yellow. Still using the dabber, add a sparkle of Light Buttermilk on each cherry. Using the no. 1 liner and Burnt Umber, paint the stems into the cherry throats.

Nest

1 Use a no. 8 flat to base the outside of the nest with Burnt Umber and the inside with Animal Black (see page 6). Use two coats for opaque coverage. Let dry.

2 Redampen the nest with gel retarder. Still using the flat, darken the bottom of the nest with Animal Black. Lighten the top of the nest with Burnt Sienna.

3 To add different color twigs, you can use the chisel edge of the floral brush or a no. 1 liner or both. Begin with Burnt Sienna. Switch to True Ochre and then Moon Yellow. Finally, add a few Arbor Green twigs. Keep the front of the nest lighter in value, which will make the nest look round.

Hydrangea

Pull petal strokes toward the center of the florets, but leave the floret centers unpainted.

1 Base in the large cluster with a no. 8 flat and two coats of Dioxazine Purple. Let dry.

2 Redampen with gel retarder. Using a floral brush, load first Dioxazine Purple (base color) and tip in Light Buttermilk, lightly brush-mixing. Paint florets of three to five petals in random placement. Let dry.

3 Redampen the flower with retarder. Use the same brush-loading method as in step 2, but this time add a bit more Light Buttermilk. Add more petals, offsetting them from the petals beneath, so more florets are created. Let dry.

4 Redampen the flower with retarder and further lighten by adding more Light Buttermilk.

For the stem, flat surface double load a floral brush with Antique Green and Black Green. Paint with the chisel edge.

5 Add centers of True Ochre, using the wood end of a liner or other small brush.

Daisy

1 Use a no. 8 flat to base the petals in Light Buttermilk, the center in Deep Burgundy and the stem in Hauser Medium Green. Use two coats of all colors for opaque coverage. Let dry.

2 Dampen the flower petals with gel retarder. Load Mix 1 (see page 6) on the dabber brush, wipe the excess paint and apply shadow values, blending down each petal. Dampen the center with retarder. Darken the bottom of the center with Black Plum on a dabber. Wipe the brush and blend where the Deep Burgundy and Black Plum meet. Let the entire flower dry.

3 Redampen the flower with retarder. Still using the dabber, further deepen the shadows with Black Green. Add touches of True Ochre in each petal. Lighten the top of the center with True Red. With a no. 1 liner, put a tiny amount of Deep Burgundy at the depression on each petal's tip. Let the flower dry completely.

4 Redampen the flower with retarder. Using Light Buttermilk on the dabber, lighten the center of the petals, not allowing the light value in the shadow areas. Double load a no. 4 flat with Cadmium Yellow and True Red. Turn the brush on the chisel edge with Cadmium Yellow at the top and push the brush upward in short staggered strokes on the unshaded portion of the flower center. You may want to add Black Green shading to the right side of the stem.

BLACK-CAPPED CHICKADEE

The tiny chickadee was my first choice to paint, and I also felt that this would be a good beginning project. The male and female chickadees are alike in appearance, their small black heads making them easy to identify.

They're very busy little characters, eating sunflower seeds and hopping from step to step on my feeder. I felt particularly blessed when my geraniums began to bloom and I was able to watch these little thieves pick off the tiny buds and quickly fly away. I assumed they were building their nest, and I wished I could follow them to see that wonderful new home, created with patience and love for their young.

Bird Materials

Paint: Acrylic, DecoArt Americana

Light Buttermilk	Moon Yellow

True Ochre	Burnt Sienna

Animal Black: Burnt Umber + Lamp Black (2:1)	Mix 1: Light Buttermilk + Animal Black (2:1)	Mix 2: Light Buttermilk + Animal Black (3:1)

Surface
• 11" x 14" (27.9cm x 35.6cm) acid-free mounting board

Brushes
Loew-Cornell
• no. 8 flat
• no. 1 liner

Nancy Kinney Specialty
• small dabber
• floral

Other
• old scruffy brush for gel retarder
• 2-inch (51mm) wash for varnishing

Additional Supplies
• Jo Sonja's Gel Retarder • paper towels for wiping brush
• J. W. etc.'s Right-Step Water Base Clear Varnish (Satin)

This pattern may be hand-traced or photocopied for personal use only. Enlarge at 200 percent to bring up to full size.

Background Materials

Paint: Acrylic, DecoArt Americana
  Background: French Vanilla, True Ochre, Raw Sienna
  Branch: Mix 1 (See bird colors.), Mix 2 (See bird colors.)

Brushes
- 2- to 4-inch (51mm to 102mm) sponge roller for basecoating
- 1-inch (25mm) wash
- no. 1 liner
- no. 8 flat
- old scruffy

Additional Supplies
- gel retarder

1 Paint the background of your choice as described in chapter 3. I used a twiggy branch on a blended-color surface. Transfer the bird pattern.

Most bird basecoating can be done with a no. 8 flat, but if you have trouble in the smaller areas, change to a smaller flat or liner. Chisel the adjoining feather areas into each other as you go (see page 10 for explanation of chiseling). Apply your basecoat colors in this order: Mix 1 on tail and wing; Animal Black on the neck, the top of the head and the eye; Light Buttermilk on the breast and cheek; Mix 1 on the beak; True Ochre on the belly and rump; Animal Black on the feet. In this photo you see the eye-ring and the top and bottom beak separation. Instructions for these are in step 3.

2 Dip the old scruffy brush into the gel retarder. Blot the excess on a paper towel and dampen the tail and wing area. Side load a no. 8 flat with Mix 2 and slide this edge down the left side of the left tail feather, creating a C-stroke at the tip. Edge all the tail feathers in this manner, starting on the right for the right feathers. Pull two long lines to paint the wing feather separations, using Mix 2. The paint in your side-loaded brush should face the outer edge of the wing. As you come to the end of the stroke, gently lift off on the brush to get a nice ending. Let dry.

Dampen the head and breast with gel. With Mix 2 on a small dabber, lightly dab the top middle of the head to lighten. Wipe your brush on a paper towel and lightly dab or rub the edges to the left and right to soften. You can always pick up Animal Black to aid in blending.

3 Again with Mix 2 on the dabber, apply paint to the middle of the black neck area. Wipe the brush and soften by dabbing or lightly rubbing up and down. If this light spot is too intense, add Animal Black to aid in a soft blending.

With Mix 2 on the no. 1 liner, lighten the top half of the beak. Flatten the liner in Animal Black and separate the top and bottom portions of the beak. Pick up Mix 2 and paint the eye-ring. Add very short lines of Animal Black at the front and back corners of the eye-ring. At the 2 o'clock position of the pupil, place a dot of Light Buttermilk for a highlight sparkle. Let dry.

4 Dampen the white areas with gel, extending into the True Ochre area. Load the dabber with Mix 1 and begin to paint in the shadows in the white areas. Start at the bottom of the beak, extending under the eye, to the side of the head and on down. Wipe the brush. Soften the Mix 1 shading into the white neck. If the mix is too intense, add Light Buttermilk. Be sure to chisel Mix 1 into the black areas to soften.

Apply Mix 2 with a dabber under the black neck. Wipe the brush and soften. This photo shows Mix 1 on the breast before softening.

5 Using the dabber, apply Burnt Sienna shadow above and below the branch on the rump and belly. Wipe the brush and soften upwards above the branch and downward below the branch. The darkest area is the rump, next to the branch. Let dry.

6 You're now ready to build up your lights and darks. This is also called glazing. Dampen the black areas with gel. Throughout this step you will use Mix 2 on the chisel edge of the floral brush. First lighten the tail and wing feather separations. Then further lighten the top of the head. Wipe the brush and soften forward and backward. Pull several downward strokes to further lighten the black neck. Wipe the brush and soften up and down. This photo shows the chest strokes before softening.

7 Dampen the white areas, the belly and the rump with gel. Load the floral with Burnt Sienna and further darken above and below the branch. Wipe the brush and soften upwards above the branch and downward below the branch. With the chisel edge of the floral, apply Light Buttermilk above the black neck. Add a tiny bit of True Ochre and blend. Reload with Light Buttermilk and apply it to the lower area of the white chest, following the feather growth direction. Wipe and blend. Lighten the belly just below the white area with Moon Yellow on the chisel of the floral. Blend.

Feet are based in with Animal Black. Dampen with the gel. Using the liner, lighten the toes with Mix 2. Paint in the claws with Animal Black.

8 Let the painting dry completely and then varnish according to the directions on page 9.

Project 2 TUFTED TITMOUSE

This busy little character is one of my favorites to watch at the feeder. He doesn't realize how small he is. I enjoy him because he thinks big.

He usually comes with his mate and then constantly darts from feeder to limb, taking quick looks for safety. He's right on any large bird that tries to land at the feeder, fussing at him with feathers all fluffed out. To my amazement, the big birds all fly away. Then this small fellow and his partner finish their fair share of the seeds and fly off to their nest.

Bird Materials

Paint: Acrylic, DecoArt Americana

Light Buttermilk

True Ochre

Animal Black:
Burnt Umber +
Lamp Black (2:1)

Mix 1: Light
Buttermilk +
Animal Black (2:1)

Mix 2: Light
Buttermilk +
Animal Black (3:1)

Surface
- 11" x 14" (27.9cm x 35.6cm) acid-free mounting board

Brushes

Loew-Cornell
- nos. 4 & 8 flats
- no. 1 liner

Nancy Kinney Specialty
- small dabber
- floral

Other
- old scruffy brush for gel retarder
- 2-inch (51mm) wash for varnishing

Additional Supplies
- Jo Sonja's Gel Retarder
- paper towels for wiping brush
- J. W. etc.'s Right-Step Water Base Clear Varnish (Satin)

This pattern may be hand-traced or photocopied for personal use only. Enlarge at 200 percent to bring up to full size.

Background Materials

Paint: Acrylic, DecoArt Americana

Background: Moon Yellow, Light Buttermilk, Raw Sienna, Burnt Sienna

Branch: Burnt Umber, Animal Black (See bird colors.)

Brushes

- 2- to 4-inch (51mm to 102mm) sponge roller for basecoating
- 1-inch (25mm) wash
- no. 1 liner
- no. 8 flat
- old scruffy

Additional Supplies

- gel retarder

1 Paint the background of your choice as described in chapter 3. I used a twiggy branch on a blended-color surface. Transfer the bird pattern.

Most bird basecoating can be done with a no. 8 flat, but if you have trouble in the smaller areas, change to a smaller flat or liner. Chisel the adjoining feather areas into each other as you go (see page 10 for explanation of chiseling). Apply your basecoat colors in this order: Mix 1 on the tail, wing, top of head and beak; Light Buttermilk on the remainder of the body; Animal Black on the eye and feet.

Tufted Titmouse, continued

2 Let the bird dry. Then dip an old scruffy brush into the gel retarder. Wipe the excess on a paper towel and dampen the gray areas. You will now shade the dark gray areas with Animal Black on the dabber. Always wipe the brush before blending. Shade under the wing where it crosses the tail. Wipe the brush and pull the black toward the bottom of the tail with the chisel edge. Blend in the same direction. Then paint a separation line between the wing and the back. Blend toward the back. Chisel shading on the wing edge that is under the neck and beside the breast. Blend into the wing. To shade the crown, start chiseling at the beak, continuing over the eye and on back to the neck. Wipe the brush and lightly blend upward.

Now you'll shade the light gray areas. First dampen these areas with gel. Remember always to wipe the brush before blending. Load Mix 1 on the dabber and start shading at the beak, moving around the eye. Blend toward the back of the head. Shade under the beak and down the front of the body. Blend into the body. Shade under the wing along the belly. Blend into the belly. Shade the rump, chiseling back into the belly. Blend toward the tail.

Corner load a no. 4 flat with Animal Black and paint a shadow where the beak is attached to the head. Wipe the brush and chisel toward the head. Blend the other edge toward the tip of the beak. Separate the beak top from the bottom using the chisel edge of the brush. Let the entire bird dry.

3 Dampen the entire bird. Double load the floral with Mix 2 and Animal Black. Paint tail-feather separations using the chisel edge. Use the same method to paint wing-feather separations, using a V-stroke. Side load the brush with Mix 2, and paint staggered C-shaped separations on the upper wing.

Now you will lighten, using the same brush, always wiping it before blending. Lighten the top and back side of the head with Mix 2. Blend the top of the head forward and backward and the side of the head up and down.

Now load with Light Buttermilk. Using the chisel edge, lighten above the eye, chiseling into the gray area, moving around the eye and to the side of the head. Blend toward the eye. You will also want to lighten the edge of the neck that overlaps the wing. Then lighten the breast, using the chisel edge of the floral. Blend down into the body and up toward the neck. Next, lighten the rump, chiseling into the shaded rump area. Blend toward the tail.

Load the floral with True Ochre and brush back and forth on the belly. Also brush a small amount in the cheek area. Lighten the top of the beak with Light Buttermilk, using a no. 4 flat. Let the bird dry.

4 Further build the lights and darks as necessary. Use Light Buttermilk on the top of the head, on the cheek and on the breast. Use Animal Black on the darker areas.

Paint the eye and feet details with a no. 1 liner. Use Mix 2 for the eye-ring. Add a Light Buttermilk sparkle at 10 o'clock. To add depth around the eye, further darken with Mix 1.

Flatten the liner in Animal Black and side load with Mix 2. With Mix 2 facing left, paint along the left edge of the toes. Repaint the claws in Animal Black if necessary.

Let the painting dry completely and then varnish according to the directions on page 9.

AMERICAN GOLDFINCH

Neighborhood yards come alive when summer arrives. For proof, look no further than this male American goldfinch decked out in his sunny summer plumage. I'll never forget the summer day I was walking my dogs when a small dash of yellow landed on a limb just in front of us. With his head held high, he sang to beat the band. I stopped and stood there in amazement as he just continued his song. The dogs were unmoved, but they stood patiently, wondering what the hold up was.

Bird Materials

Paint: Acrylic, DecoArt Americana

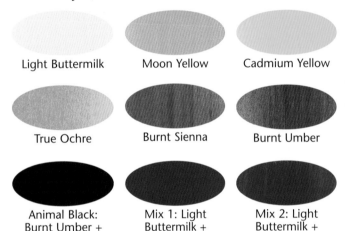

Light Buttermilk	Moon Yellow	Cadmium Yellow
True Ochre	Burnt Sienna	Burnt Umber
Animal Black: Burnt Umber + Lamp Black (2:1)	Mix 1: Light Buttermilk + Animal Black (2:1)	Mix 2: Light Buttermilk + Animal Black (3:1)

Surface
• 11" x 14" (27.9cm x 35.6cm) acid-free mounting board

Brushes
Loew-Cornell
• nos. 4 & 8 flats
• no. 1 liner

Nancy Kinney Specialty
• small dabber
• floral

Other
• old scruffy brush for gel retarder
• 2-inch (51mm) wash for varnishing

Additional Supplies
• Jo Sonja's Gel Retarder
• J. W. etc.'s Right-Step Water Base Clear Varnish (Satin)
• paper towels for wiping brush

This pattern may be hand-traced or photocopied for personal use only. Enlarge at 264 percent to bring up to full size.

Background Materials

Paint: Acrylic, DecoArt Americana

Background: Antique Green, Black Green, Celery Green

Branch: Fawn, Animal Black (See bird colors.)

Brushes
- 2- to 4-inch (51mm to 102mm) sponge roller for basecoating
- no. 8 flat
- no. 1 liner
- old scruffy

Additional Supplies
- plastic wrap
- paper towel
- gel retarder
- sea sponge
- spray mist water bottle

1 Paint the background with two coats of Antique Green as described in chapter 3. I used a birch branch with the sponge-and-plastic wrap surface technique. Transfer the bird pattern.

Most basecoating of the bird can be done with a no. 8 flat, but if you have trouble in the smaller areas, change to a smaller flat or liner. Chisel the adjoining feather areas into each other as you go (see page 10 for an explanation of chiseling). Apply your basecoat colors in this order: Animal Black on tail, wings, top of head and eye; Light Buttermilk on the rump; True Ochre on the beak and remainder of the body. In this photo I'm chiseling the True Ochre into the wing.

Also, in this photo you see the beak separation and the eye details. The beak separation is a faint pattern line. Instructions for the eye come later.

2 Let the bird dry. Then dip an old scruffy brush into the gel retarder. Wipe the excess on a paper towel and dampen the tail, wings and top of the head. Using the chisel edge of the dabber with Mix 2, lighten the tail tips. Wipe the brush and blend upwards to lightly separate the two tail feathers. Apply Light Buttermilk on the tail feather tips with the chisel of the dabber.

Still using the dabber, lighten the outer edge of both wings with Mix 2. Wipe the brush and blend the inner edges. On the left wing, indicate feather separations with staggered C-stokes of Light Buttermilk.

Apply Mix 2 in the middle of the head with the dabber. Wipe the brush and blend to the left and right. Use a little Animal Black to soften the edges if necessary.

3 Apply gel to all yellow areas and the white rump. Use the dabber to chisel a Mix 1 shadow into the rump. Then chisel Burnt Sienna from the top of the head, around the eye, and into and under the beak. Wipe the brush and blend into the yellow area. When blending under the beak, extend the Burnt Sienna along the neckline to indicate the turning of the head. Shade above and below the branch with the same color—no chiseling necessary. Wipe the brush and blend above the branch upward and below the branch downward. Then chisel Burnt Sienna where the beak is attached to the head. Wipe the brush and blend into the beak. Let dry.

4 Dampen the rump, the yellow sections and the top of the head with gel. Strengthen the rump shadow with Mix 2, using the floral. Lighten the outer tip of the rump with Light Buttermilk, using the chisel edge of the floral.

Strengthen the beak shadows with Burnt Umber, using the chisel edge of the no. 4 flat. Separate the top and bottom beak halves with Burnt Umber on the no. 1 liner. With the same brush, apply Animal Black from the beak tip slightly back toward the head. Lighten the upper beak half with a tiny amount of Cadmium Yellow. Using Burnt Umber on the floral, build shadow areas around the beak, chiseling into the beak, and then around the eye and into the back of the head. Lightly pull the color into the side of the head. Still using Burnt Umber on the floral, deepen under the beak, above the branch and below the branch. Wipe the brush and blend above the branch upward and below the branch downward.

Let dry and redampen with gel. With Cadmium Yellow on the floral, lighten the yellow areas at the side of the head and across the breast, using the chisel edge. Let dry and redampen. Further lighten the same areas with Moon Yellow.

5 Double load a flattened no. 1 liner with True Ochre and Animal Black. Paint the toes in C-strokes. Paint Animal Black claws with the no. 1 liner, using short comma-like strokes.

6 Paint the eye details with a no. 1 liner. Use Cadmium Yellow for the eye-ring. Add a Moon Yellow highlight on top of the eye-ring above and below the pupil. Add a Light Buttermilk sparkle at 11 o'clock and a smaller sparkle at 5 o'clock.

7 Allow the painting to dry completely and then varnish according to the directions on page 9.

As fall sets in, most of the birds I've been feeding migrate south. How sad to glance out to a full feeder with no bird activity. I find comfort knowing that with the first snow come the small Junco flocks, also known as snowbirds. Are they out there all along, just waiting for the first flakes to fall? When that happens, they dance over the white snow, chirping and cracking seeds as they bring life back to the feeder. As the winter snows melt, these small birds migrate from the Carolinas as far north as Alaska. When fall comes, I'll have the feeder full, waiting for their return.

Bird Materials

Paint: Acrylic, DecoArt Americana

Light Buttermilk

Moon Yellow

Burnt Umber

Animal Black:
Burnt Umber +
Lamp Black (2:1)

Mix 1: Light
Buttermilk +
Animal Black (2:1)

Mix 2: Light
Buttermilk +
Animal Black (3:1)

Surface
• 11" x 14" (27.9cm x 35.6cm) acid-free mounting board

Brushes
Loew-Cornell
• no. 8 flat
• no. 1 liner

Nancy Kinney Specialty
• small dabber
• floral

Other
• old scruffy brush for gel retarder
• 2-inch (51mm) wash for varnishing

Additional Supplies
• Jo Sonja's Gel Retarder • paper towels for wiping brush
• J. W. etc.'s Right-Step Water Base Clear Varnish (Satin)

Background Materials

Paint: Acrylic, DecoArt Americana
Background: Celery Green, Moon Yellow, True Ochre, Antique Green

Branch: Asphaltum, Black Green

Brushes
• 2- to 4-inch (51mm to 102mm) sponge roller for basecoating
• 1-inch (25mm) wash   • no. 8 flat
• old scruffy   • floral

Additional Supplies
• gel retarder

This pattern may be hand-traced or photocopied for personal use only. Enlarge at 200 percent to bring up to full size.

1 Paint the background of your choice as explained in chapter 3. I used a pine branch on a blended-color surface. Transfer the bird pattern.

Most bird basecoating can be done with a no. 8 flat, but if you have trouble in the smaller areas, change to a smaller flat or liner. Chisel the adjoining feather areas into each other as you go (see page 10 for explanation of chiseling). Apply your basecoat colors in this order: Mix 1 on the tail; Animal Black on the left side of the body; Mix 1 on the primary wing and then the secondary wing; Animal Black on the breast, head and back; Moon Yellow on the beak; Light Buttermilk on the belly and rump; Animal Black on the eye.

In this photo I'm chiseling the Light Buttermilk on the belly. Also in this photo you see that I have separated the top and bottom beak halves with Burnt Umber on a no. 1 liner, which can be done anytime the beak is dry.

2 Let the bird dry. Then dip an old scruffy brush into the gel retarder. Blot the excess on a paper towel and dampen the tail and wings. With Mix 2 on the dabber, lighten the bottom edge of the tail. Wipe the brush on a paper towel and blend upwards. Use the chisel of the floral to separate the tail feathers in Animal Black.

With Mix 2 on the dabber, lighten the primary and secondary wing. Flat surface double load the floral in Animal Black and Mix 1. Using the floral chisel edge with Mix 1 facing the belly, paint wing feather separations in elongated C-strokes.

3 Dampen the head and breast areas with gel. Use a dabber to apply Mix 2 to the top of the head, above the eye. Wipe the brush and blend to the right and the left. Apply Mix 2 to the back of the head with the chisel edge of the dabber. Wipe the brush and blend upwards. Using the same method, lighten the cheek area from the beak down and around. Blend toward the eye. Lighten the breast across the middle, chiseling up and down. Wipe the brush and blend up and down. Finally, chisel Mix 2 toward the secondary wing and on down. If any of the light values seem too intense, you can add the base color to soften the edges and aid in blending. Let dry.

4 **(See photo of completed bird on page 38.)** Dampen the white belly and rump with gel. Using Mix 2 on the dabber, chisel from the white upper belly into the black breast. Then chisel from above the branch into the rump to create a shadow. Wipe the brush and soften both areas toward the middle of the belly. Shade the beak in Burnt Umber where it meets the head.

Now you can further lighten the dark areas and shade the light areas, using the same colors and brushes. Be sure the area you want to work on has been dampened with the gel. When you're done shading the belly, lighten its middle with Light Buttermilk, using the chisel edge of the floral.

Using a no. 1 liner, paint the eye-ring in Mix 2 and a Light Buttermilk sparkle at 2 o'clock. Then once the bird is dry, you can add the parts of the branch that cross in front of the bird. Let the painting dry completely and then varnish according to the directions on page 9.

A sense of spring is definitely in the air when you see that first dash of blue darting erratically across the yard. I believe the beautiful bluebird is designed for our enjoyment, just as the old cliché, "bluebird of happiness," suggests.

The bluebird will build a nest and raise its family in a specially made box raised three or four feet from the ground. I find their instinct to build the perfect nest breathtaking. The male and female birds enjoy working together as they embellish their home for their new brood. Maybe we as humans can learn something about building our own perfect "nest" by watching the work and love demonstrated by the male and female bluebird.

Bird Materials

Paint: Acrylic, DecoArt Americana

Light Buttermilk

Moon Yellow

True Ochre

Burnt Sienna

Baby Blue

Victorian Blue

Prussian Blue

Animal Black:
Burnt Umber +
Lamp Black (2:1)

Mix 1: Light
Buttermilk +
Animal Black (2:1)

Mix 2: Light
Buttermilk +
Animal Black (3:1)

Surface
• 11" x 14" (27.9cm x 35.6cm) acid-free mounting board

Brushes
Loew-Cornell
• no. 8 flat
• no. 1 liner

Nancy Kinney Specialty
• small dabber
• floral

Other
• old scruffy brush for gel retarder
• 2-inch (51mm) wash for varnishing

Additional Supplies
• Jo Sonja's Gel Retarder   • paper towels for wiping brush
• J. W. etc.'s Right-Step Water Base Clear Varnish (Satin)

This pattern may be hand-traced or photocopied for personal use only. Enlarge at 200 percent to bring up to full size.

Background Materials

Paint: Acrylic, DecoArt Americana

Background: French Vanilla, Burnt Sienna, Raw Sienna, Antique Green

Branch: Burnt Umber, Light Buttermilk

Brushes

- 2- to 4-inch (51mm to 102mm) sponge roller for basecoating
- 1-inch (25mm) wash
- no. 8 flat
- no. 1 liner
- old scruffy

Additional Supplies

- gel retarder

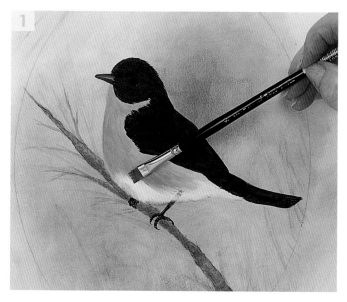

1 Paint the background of your choice as described in chapter 3. I used a birch branch on a blended-color surface. Transfer the bird pattern. I traced an oval around the bird because I anticipated using an oval mat to frame the finished painting. The background extends just a little beyond the oval. If you're not sure what matting you want to use, extend your background to the edges of the mounting board.

Most bird basecoating can be done with a no. 8 flat, but if you have trouble in the smaller areas, change to a smaller flat or liner. Chisel the adjoining feather areas into each other as you go (see page 10 for explanation of chiseling). Apply your basecoat colors in this order: Prussian Blue on the tail, wings, back and head; Light Buttermilk on the rump and belly; True Ochre on the remaining body areas; Animal Black on the eye and beak. Basecoat the feet with Mix 1. Lighten the top of the beak with Mix 2, which will give you beak separation. In this photo I'm chiseling True Ochre into the belly. Let dry.

2 Dip an old scruffy brush into the gel retarder. Blot the excess on a paper towel and dampen the blue areas. Use the dabber to apply Victorian Blue on the end of the tail. Wipe the brush and pull the color up the tail. Dab Victorian Blue on the top of the back, blending slightly up toward the bird's body. Use the same color and dab on the middle of the shoulder. Wipe the brush and pat to blend. Apply the same color to the top of the head, wipe the brush and blend to the left and right. Chisel the same blue on the cheek from the beak down around the bottom of the eye. Wipe the brush and blend slightly back toward the eye.

Changing to the floral brush, flat surface load one side with Victorian Blue. With your color toward the belly of the bird, use the chisel edge to paint the elongated C-stroke to indicate feather separations on the wing.

3 Dampen the white area with gel. Using the dabber, apply Mix 2 along the bottom edge back toward the tail. Wipe the brush and blend upward with the chisel edge. Now apply Burnt Sienna from the bottom of the beak down the outside of the belly and a little on top of the white area. Do the same under the bird's blue cheek. Using the chisel edge of the dabber, add choppy, staggered strokes of Burnt Sienna on the breast area.

4 Be sure the blue areas are dry, and then dampen with gel. Use a floral to apply Baby Blue to the end of the tail. Using the dabber, pat in this same color on the top of the head, wipe the brush and blend to the left and the right. Side load your Baby Blue and add more color to the cheek. Wipe the brush and blend. Then apply the same color to the back of the wing, wipe the brush and pat to blend. Use the same technique on the center of the wing shoulder. Let dry.

5 Dampen all areas and further build the light and dark values as needed. Using the floral's chisel edge, further lighten the wing separations with Baby Blue. Shade under the lower portion of the wing and strengthen the outside edge of the belly with Burnt Sienna. Lighten the yellow breast with Moon Yellow, chiseling into the wing.

With a no. 1 liner, paint a Victorian Blue eye-ring. Add a Light Buttermilk sparkle at 11 o'clock and a smaller sparkle at 5 o'clock. Lighten the top of the beak with Mix 2.

With the no. 1 liner, paint the toes with Mix 1. While the toes remain damp, lighten the left edges with Mix 2. Paint the claws with Animal Black.

6 Let the painting dry completely and then varnish according to the directions on page 9.

Project 6 — *Indigo Bunting*

This small finch makes his home in the eastern part of the United States and Canada, living on the bushy edges of the forest. His voice is very lively. In the winter the male Indigo Bunting is more brown, resembling the female, although there are touches of strong blue. In the summer, the plumage of the male turns a breathtaking rich, deep blue all over. Can't you imagine that just-right female fluttering by, noticing the indigo's handsome majesty nestled among the leaves? I wonder if she thinks, *Is he the one?*

Bird Materials

Paint: Acrylic, DecoArt Americana

Light Buttermilk   Baby Blue

Victorian Blue   Prussian Blue   Dioxazine Purple

Animal Black: Burnt Umber + Lamp Black (2:1)   Mix 2: Light Buttermilk + Animal Black (3:1)   Mix 7: Victorian Blue + Prussian Blue (2:1)

Surface
- 11" x 14" (27.9cm x 35.6cm) acid-free mounting board

Brushes

Loew-Cornell
- nos. 8 & 12 flats
- no. 1 liner

Nancy Kinney Specialty
- small dabber
- floral

Other
- old scruffy brush for gel retarder
- 2-inch (51mm) wash for varnishing

Additional Supplies
- Jo Sonja's Gel Retarder
- paper towels for wiping brush
- J. W. etc.'s Right-Step Water Base Clear Varnish (Satin)

This pattern may be hand-traced or photocopied for personal use only. Enlarge at 182 percent to bring up to full size.

Background Materials

Paint: Acrylic, DecoArt Americana
  Background: French Grey Blue, Prussian Blue
  Leaves: Antique Green, Black Green, Celery Green

Brushes
- 2- to 4-inch (51mm to 102mm) sponge
  roller for basecoating
- no. 8 flat   • dabber
- no. 1 liner   • old scruffy

Additional Supplies
- 1-inch (25mm) diameter candle with holder
- old stainless steel tablespoon
- Krylon Matte Finish spray 1311
- gel retarder

1 Paint the background of your choice as described in chapter 3. I used green leaves and curlicues on a smoked surface. (Curlicues appear in completed bird photos on pages 44 and 47.) Transfer the bird pattern.

    Most bird basecoating can be done with a no. 8 flat, but if you have trouble in the smaller areas, change to a smaller flat or liner. Chisel the adjoining feather areas into each other as you go (see page 10 for explanation of chiseling). Apply your basecoat colors in this order: Victorian Blue on all feathered areas except the wings; Animal Black on the beak and eye; Mix 7 on the wings.

2 Let the bird dry. Then dip an old scruffy brush into the gel retarder. Wipe the excess on a paper towel and dampen the bird. Unless instructed otherwise, in this and the next step you will apply shading with Prussian Blue, using the dabber. Always remember to wipe the brush on a paper towel before blending. Start by chiseling shading on the tail, working up under the tail covert. Blend toward the tail tip. Shade under the back of the wing on the tail covert and blend slightly. Chisel shading on the bottom tail covert into the rump. Blend toward the back of the bird. Finish shading under the wing and also down the front of the belly. Blend both areas inward.

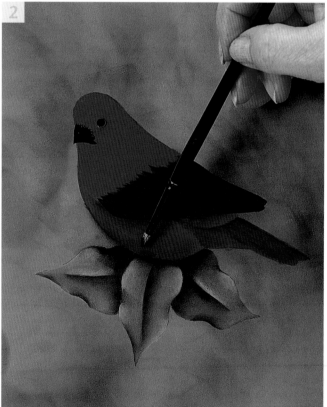

3 Continue shading the outer edge of the body up to the beak and across the lower portion of the neck with Prussian Blue. Blend downward from the beak and inward from the left edge of the body. Shade the face by chiseling into the right edge of the beak and bringing the color around the eye. Blend toward the back of the head. While this is still wet, shade the beak and under the beak with a bit of Animal Black. Let dry.

Returning to Prussian Blue, chisel shading into the cheek. Blend toward the wing. Shade down the back of the neck, blending forward and backward. With a small dab of Prussian Blue on the chisel of the dabber, draw a slight separation line between the shoulders. Let dry.

4 Redampen the bird with gel. Unless instructed otherwise, in this and the next step you will apply the light value with Baby Blue, using the floral. Always wipe the brush before blending. If the light value is too intense, pick up some Victorian Blue to aid in the blending and softening.

Lighten the upper and lower tail coverts, chiseling over the tail. Blend toward the tail tip. Lighten the rump, chiseling into the covert. Wipe the brush and continue to add Baby Blue over the belly area.

5 Lighten the back, chiseling over the wings. Blend toward the head. Lighten the cheek, chiseling toward the neck. Blend toward the eye without getting in the shading of the eye. Lighten the top of the head, blending forward and backward.

Using the chisel edge of the floral, lighten the top and bottom of the beak with Mix 2, brushing from the tip back. Using the no. 1 liner, separate the upper and lower beak halves with Animal Black.

6 Dampen the wings with gel. Using Prussian Blue on the floral, continue the shoulder separation line down between the wings. Flat surface double load the floral with Prussian Blue and Baby Blue. Using the chisel edge with Baby Blue toward the bird's body, paint elongated C-stroke feather separations. Side load the floral with Baby Blue and paint staggered C-stroke covert feather indications. Let dry.

7 Redampen the bird with gel and further build the lights and darks as necessary. To enhance your strengthening of the darks, use a no. 12 flat to apply a light wash of Dioxazine Purple around the eye, under the neck and a bit under the wing. Don't let this wash get into the light areas.

Paint the eye and feet details with a no. 1 liner. Use Victorian Blue for the eye-ring. Add a Light Buttermilk sparkle at 10 o'clock. Flatten the liner in Animal Black and side load with Mix 2. With Mix 2 facing left, apply just a hint of paint along the left edge of the claws.

Let the painting dry completely and then varnish according to the directions on page 9.

7 SNOW BUNTING

This white-winged Snow Bunting really resembles his name. I wanted to depict him surrounded in greenery, and pine branches provide just the right mood for the forecast of a snowy winter. In fact, I automatically think of snow when I look at this painting. I wonder if he's heard the weather report.

The Snow Bunting is the largest of the juncos and is most often seen in the hills of South Dakota.

Bird Materials

Paint: Acrylic, DecoArt Americana

Light Buttermilk

True Ochre

Animal Black: Burnt Umber + Lamp Black (2:1)

Mix 1: Light Buttermilk + Animal Black (2:1)

Mix 2: Light Buttermilk + Animal Black (3:1)

Surface
• 11" x 14" (27.9cm x 35.6cm) acid-free mounting board

Brushes
Loew-Cornell
• no. 8 flat
• no. 1 liner

Nancy Kinney Specialty
• small dabber
• floral

Other
• old scruffy brush for gel retarder
• 2-inch (51mm) wash for varnishing

Additional Supplies
• Jo Sonja's Gel Retarder
• J. W. etc.'s Right-Step Water Base Clear Varnish (Satin)
• paper towels for wiping brush

This pattern may be hand-traced or photocopied for personal use only. Enlarge at 189 percent to bring up to full size.

Background Materials

Paint: Acrylic, DecoArt Americana

Background: Soft Sage, Black Green

Pine Branch: Animal Black (See bird colors.), Light Buttermilk, Mix 2 (See bird colors.), Black Green

Brushes
- 2- to 4-inch (51mm to 102mm) sponge roller for basecoating
- 1-inch (25mm) wash
- floral
- no. 8 flat
- old scruffy

Additional Supplies
- gel retarder

1 Paint the background of your choice as described in chapter 3. I used a pine branch on a blended-color surface. Transfer the bird pattern.

Most bird basecoating can be done with a no. 8 flat, but if you have trouble in the smaller areas, change to a smaller flat or liner. Chisel the adjoining feather areas into each other as you go (see page 10 for explanation of chiseling). Apply your basecoat colors in this order: Light Buttermilk on all light areas; Animal Black on all dark areas. Be sure to chisel the beak into the white of the head and the white of the head into the beak. While the beak is still wet, lighten the beak top with Mix 1.

2 Let the bird dry. Then dip an old scruffy brush into the gel retarder. Wipe the excess on a paper towel and dampen the belly and rump. Using Mix 1 on the dabber, apply shading at the rump and under the wing, sliding up the wing. Fill in the rump area with Mix 1. Wipe the brush and blend up the bird's belly. Wipe the brush and work Light Buttermilk from the upper breast down to the Mix 1 area. Wipe the brush, pick up a touch of True Ochre and work it up and down in the belly area.

3 Dampen the head with gel. Using Mix 2 on the dabber, start right under the beak and work down the front of the breast, tapering into a V shape. Apply Mix 2 above the beak and around the eye. Wipe the brush and blend up into the head and around the eye. Use Light Buttermilk to aid in the softening where needed. Let dry.

4 Redampen the head with gel. Strengthen the shading with Mix 1 on the dabber, working above the beak and around the eye area. Wipe the brush and blend. Add the tiniest touch of True Ochre at the back of the head. Wipe the brush and dab lightly to blend. At any point you can add Light Buttermilk to aid in blending the two colors.

5 Using Mix 2 on the dabber, shade the white shoulder, chiseling into the breast. Wipe the brush and blend lightly down the wing. Use the chisel edge of the dabber to slide Mix 2 along the white wing feathers to separate. While Mix 2 is on the brush, lighten the black shoulder portion of the wing by lightly dabbing. Let the wing dry.

6 Redampen the wing with gel. Using the chisel edge of the floral, separate the white feathers with a thin line of Mix 1. In the same way, separate the black wing and tail feathers with Mix 2.

7 Dampen the top of the head, shoulder and breast with gel. Use the chisel edge of the floral to lighten the top of the head with Light Buttermilk. Chisel this color over the shoulder and along the top of the wing. Wipe the brush and chisel toward the eye. With the same color, lighten across the middle of the breast. Wipe the brush and blend upward and downward. Let dry.

8 Redampen the bird and further build the lights and darks as necessary.

Paint the eye details with a no. 1 liner. Use Mix 2 for the eye-ring. If the eye-ring doesn't show, lightly outline it with Mix 1, using the liner. Add a Light Buttermilk sparkle at 2 o'clock. Then side load the liner with Mix 2 and paint a light C-stroke from 9 o 'clock to 5 o'clock to indicate the pupil.

Let the painting dry completely and then varnish according to the directions on page 9.

Project 8
VERMILION FLYCATCHER

Most flycatchers are drab in color. One only has to look once to see that the vermilion flycatcher is definitely the exception—and a very striking creation. The male is a real eye-catcher with his bright red head and under parts. The female is gray-brown with a whitish forehead and eyebrow and a black tail. She has just a wash of pink on her white breast and tail. These beautiful flycatchers are seen year round in the southwest United States.

Bird Materials

Paint: Acrylic, DecoArt Americana

Light Buttermilk	Cadmium Yellow
True Red	Deep Burgundy
Black Plum	Fawn
	Burnt Umber
Animal Black: Burnt Umber + Lamp Black (2:1)	Mix 2: Light Buttermilk + Animal Black (3:1)
	Mix 5: Burnt Umber + touch of Animal Black

Surface
• 11" x 14" (27.9cm x 35.6cm) acid-free mounting board

Brushes
Loew-Cornell
• no. 8 flat
• no. 1 liner

Nancy Kinney Specialty
• small dabber
• floral

Other
• old scruffy brush for gel retarder
• 2-inch (51mm) wash for varnishing

Additional Supplies
• Jo Sonja's Gel Retarder
• J. W. etc.'s Right-Step Water Base Clear Varnish (Satin)
• paper towels for wiping brush

This pattern may be hand-traced or photocopied for personal use only. Enlarge at 238 percent to bring up to full size.

Background Materials

Paint: Acrylic, DecoArt Americana

  Background: Driftwood, Deep Burgundy

  Grass: Antique Green, Deep Burgundy

Brushes

- 2- to 4-inch (51mm to 102mm) sponge roller for basecoating
- 1-inch (25mm) wash   • no. 1 liner
- old scruffy

Additional Supplies

- 1-inch (25mm) diameter candle with holder
- old stainless steel tablespoon
- Krylon Matte Finish spray 1311
- gel retarder

1 Paint the background of your choice as described in chapter 3. I used grass on a blended-color and smoked surface. The sea grass is painted using the no. 1 liner with a brush mix of Antique Green + a touch of Deep Burgundy. Paint in loose, long, irregular strokes creating grass stems. Add tiny smudges of this color to the stem tops to represent sea oats. Transfer the bird pattern.

Most bird basecoating can be done with a no. 8 flat, but if you have trouble in the smaller areas, change to a smaller flat or liner. Chisel the adjoining feather areas into each other as you go (see page 10 for explanation of chiseling). Apply your basecoat colors in this order: Deep Burgundy on all the red areas; Mix 5 on the brown areas; Animal Black on the beak, eye and feet. Beak and feet details seen in this photo are explained in step 3.

Vermilion Flycatcher, continued

2 Let the bird dry. Then dip an old scruffy brush into the gel retarder. Blot the excess on a paper towel and then dampen the tail. Very slightly lighten the tail with a little Fawn on the dabber. Then load one flat side of the floral with Fawn and use the chisel edge to paint tail feather separations in elongated C-strokes. Dampen the remainder of the brown areas with gel and paint the primary wing separation lines in the same manner. Load the no. 8 flat with Burnt Umber and then side load with a little Fawn. With the Fawn facing the primary wing, paint the bottom row of short C-strokes on the secondary wing.

With Animal Black on the dabber, add shading at the beak base, blending back toward the eye. Shade around the eye, chiseling into the red cap. Then shade under the cheek, wipe the brush and blend out toward the wing. Finally, apply shading under the back coverts that lay over the primary wing, slightly blending downward. Now lighten the covert edges with Fawn, using the chisel edge of the dabber.

Side load the no. 8 flat with Fawn and add a row of jagged C-strokes above the short C-strokes you've already painted. On the neck, paint staggered Vs, starting the strokes at the point. Make the Vs smaller as you work toward the head.

3 Dampen the red areas with gel. With Black Plum on the dabber, chisel toward the beak and around the top of the eye. Wipe the brush and blend toward the top of the head. Chisel Black Plum at the back of the head. Wipe the brush and blend toward the top of the head. Chisel Black Plum under the beak and in a long streak under the eye. Wipe the brush and blend toward the back. Shade with Black Plum under the wing. Wipe the brush and soften the outer edge. Shade under the neck, down the front of the body, over the leg and up to the tail covert. Wipe the brush and lightly rub to blend. Let everything dry.

With the dabber, lighten across the top of the head with True Red. Wipe the brush and blend toward the front and the back. With the floral, chisel in True Red to lighten over the cheek area. Lighten the belly and rump, starting to chisel in the middle and extending to the tail-feather covert.

Use the floral to brush-mix Cadmium Yellow + True Red to a light orange. Lighten the top of the head with the chisel edge. Wipe the brush and blend to the back and to the front. Then lighten the cheek area, chiseling over the brown area. Use True Red to add a bit of light value to the belly and the lower edge of the tail covert.

Use the no. 1 liner for the beak, feet and eye details. Lighten the beak top with Mix 2. Load the liner in Animal Black and side load with Mix 2 and paint short curved strokes across the toes. Paint the claws with Animal Black. Paint the eye-ring with Mix 2 and the sparkle with Light Buttermilk at 11 o'clock.

Let the painting dry completely and then varnish according to the directions on page 9.

When these sparrows migrate south from Canada in the winter, birders argue about just what these birds are singing. Our Canada neighbors say the birds sing, "Oh Canada, Oh sweet Canada." People in the states say they're singing, "Here I come again." Announcing their arrival with their beautiful song, the flocks settle in gardens and backyards, adding a note of cheer to dreary winter days.

Bird Materials

Paint: Acrylic, DecoArt Americana

Light Buttermilk

Cadmium Yellow

Moon Yellow

Fawn

Burnt Umber

Animal Black:
Burnt Umber +
Lamp Black (2:1)

Mix 1: Light
Buttermilk +
Animal Black (2:1)

Mix 2: Light
Buttermilk +
Animal Black (3:1)

Surface
• 11" x 14" (27.9cm x 35.6cm) acid-free mounting board

Brushes
Loew-Cornell
• nos. 4 & 8 flats
• no. 1 liner

Nancy Kinney Specialty
• small dabber
• floral

Other
• old scruffy brush for gel retarder
• 2-inch (51mm) wash for varnishing

Additional Supplies
• Jo Sonja's Gel Retarder   • paper towels for wiping brush
• J. W. etc.'s Right-Step Water Base Clear Varnish (Satin)

This pattern may be hand-traced or photocopied for personal use only. Enlarge at 182 percent to bring up to full size.

Background Materials

Paint: Acrylic, DecoArt Americana

Background: Silver Sage Green, Moon Yellow, Light Buttermilk, Prussian Blue, Black Green

Branches and leaves: Antique Green, Black Green, Cadmium Yellow, Moon Yellow

Brushes

- 2- to 4-inch (51mm to 102mm) sponge roller for basecoating
- 1-inch (25mm) wash
- no. 8 flat
- dabber
- old scruffy

Additional Supplies

- gel retarder

1 Paint the background of your choice as described in chapter 3. I used green leaves on a blended-color surface. Transfer the bird pattern.

Most bird basecoating can be done with a no. 8 flat, but if you have trouble in the smaller areas, change to a smaller flat or liner. Chisel the adjoining feather areas into each other as you go (see page 10 for explanation of chiseling). Apply your basecoat colors in this order: Mix 2 on the tail, breast, cheek and beak; Burnt Umber on the wings; Light Buttermilk on the breast, throat and light head stripes; Cadmium Yellow on the yellow head patch; Animal Black on the dark head stripes and the eye.

2 Let the bird dry. Then dip an old scruffy brush into the gel retarder. Wipe the excess on a paper towel and dampen the tail and wing. Using Animal Black on the dabber, shade the tail around the leaves and the rump. Wipe the brush and blend down the tail. Shade the top of the right wing, chiseling into the shoulder and bringing the color down the left edge of the wing. Wipe the brush and blend down the wing. On the left wing, chisel shading into the breast and the black head stripe. (Only an edge of this wing is seen, below the head and to the left of the breast.) Wipe the brush and blend. Wipe the brush and pick up a small amount of Mix 2 on the chisel edge. Pointing the dabber to the outer edge of each wing, lightly blur the outside edges. This creates the illusion of roundness to the bird.

3 Flat surface load the no. 8 flat with Light Buttermilk. Starting at the right tail tip with the paint facing the middle of the tail, swing up while gently lifting. Do a couple more feather separations on the right side of the tail. Then turn the brush and paint feather separations on the left side of the tail.

4 Make sure the wing is dry and then redampen it with gel. Flat surface double load the floral with Fawn and Animal Black. Paint the three rows of wing feather separations with the Fawn side of the brush facing the bird body.

5 Dampen the remainder of the bird. With the dabber and Mix 2, shade behind the leaves on the belly. With Mix 1 on the brush, pick up a tiny amount of Moon Yellow and blend the shading up into the breast. Using Mix 1 on the dabber, shade down the left side of the gray breast and under the eye. Chisel shading into the beak and under the black band over the right wing. Still using the dabber, shade the white areas of the head with Mix 1 and the yellow areas with Burnt Umber. Wipe the brush and blend.

Using the no. 4 flat, shade the beak with Animal Black. Use the chisel edge to paint a separation line between the upper and lower halves of the beak.

Using the dabber and Mix 1, blur the top edge of the head as you did the wing edges at the end of step 2. Let the bird dry.

6 Redampen the bird with gel. Using Light Buttermilk on the floral, lighten the gray breast, chiseling a bit into the right wing. Lighten the white head bar, just to the left of the eye. Then lighten the top half of the beak. Still using the floral, lighten the left edge of the yellow head patch with Cadmium Yellow. Using the no. 1 liner, reinforce the edges of the black areas on the head. Let dry.

7 Redampen the bird with gel and further build the lights and darks as necessary. Use Light Buttermilk on the light areas and Mix 1 on the dark areas.

Paint the eye details with a no. 1 liner. Paint the eye-ring with Mix 2. Flatten the liner in Animal Black and side load in Mix 2. Paint small C-strokes on the left and right edges of the pupil. Add a Light Buttermilk sparkle at 2 o'clock.

Let the painting dry completely and then varnish according to the directions on page 9.

RUFUS-SIDED TOWHEE

A shiny black male towhee frequently visits my feeder with his female. One of the most interesting things about this bird is his red eyes. He's often mistaken for the robin, but those red eyes distinguish between the two. The white tail corners are also good identification marks.

The male towhee does not hesitate to run larger birds, such as cardinals or blue jays, from the feeder. He sure protects his female!

Bird Materials

Paint: Acrylic, DecoArt Americana

Light Buttermilk	True Ochre	Burnt Sienna
Animal Black: Burnt Umber + Lamp Black (2:1)	Mix 3: Animal Black + Prussian Blue (3:1)	Mix 4: Light Buttermilk + touch of Mix 3

Surface
• 11" x 14" (27.9cm x 35.6cm) acid-free mounting board

Brushes
Loew-Cornell
• no. 8 flat
• no. 1 liner

Nancy Kinney Specialty
• small dabber
• floral

Other
• old scruffy brush for gel retarder
• 2-inch (51mm) wash for varnishing

Additional Supplies
• Jo Sonja's Gel Retarder
• J. W. etc.'s Right-Step Water Base Clear Varnish (Satin)
• paper towels for wiping brush

This pattern may be hand-traced or photocopied for personal use only. Enlarge at 222 percent to bring up to full size.

Background Materials

Paint: Acrylic, DecoArt Americana

Background: Driftwood, Prussian Blue, Lamp Black

Branch, leaves and curlicues: Antique Green, Black Green, Celery Green, Light Buttermilk, Mix 4 (See bird colors.), Burnt Sienna

Brushes
- 2- to 4-inch (51mm to 102mm) sponge roller for basecoating
- no. 8 flat
- dabber
- no. 1 liner
- old scruffy

Additional Supplies
- plastic wrap
- spray mist water bottle
- large sea sponge
- gel retarder

1 Paint the background of your choice as described in chapter 3. I did this painting two ways. Both have a branch-and-leaves design, but one background is done with sponge and plastic wrap (pages 60 and 63) and the other just sponged (pages 61 and 62). You can add curlicues (see page 15) either now or after the bird is finished. Transfer the bird pattern.

Most bird basecoating can be done with a no. 8 flat, but if you have trouble in the smaller areas, change to a smaller flat or liner. Chisel the adjoining feather areas into each other as you go (see page 10 for explanation of chiseling). Apply your basecoat colors in this order: Mix 3 on the tail's dark parts; Light Buttermilk on the tail's light parts, keeping a slight separation of the six feathers; Light Buttermilk on the two outside tail feather edges, painting with the chisel edge; Mix 3 on the wing, breast, eye and head; Burnt Sienna in the red areas; Light Buttermilk on the belly, rump and leg puff; Mix 3 on the feet and beak, leaving a fine line between beak halves.

2 Let the bird dry. Then dip an old scruffy brush into the gel retarder. Blot the excess on a paper towel and dampen the tail. Use Mix 4 on the dabber to shade under the ends of the tail feathers, starting with the lower feathers and working up. Chisel in Mix 4 where the white part of the tail feathers meets the upper black part, and continue down on the outside edges of the tail feathers. Wipe the brush and lightly blend downward. With Mix 3 on the no. 1 liner, separate the white portions of the tail-feather sections down the middle.

Use the dabber to apply a tiny amount of Mix 4 on the black portion of the tail feathers. Wipe the brush and blend downward. With Mix 4 on the liner, separate the black portions of the tail feather sections down the middle. With the same color, use the dabber tip to lighten the black tip edge of the right tail feather to separate it from the left. Using the chisel of the no. 8 flat, strengthen the two outer edges of the tail feathers using Light Buttermilk. Let dry.

RUFUS-SIDED TOWHEE, continued

3 Dampen the wing, breast, head and beak with gel. Using the dabber and Mix 4, lighten the outer edge of the wing, working from the wing tip up to the side of the head. Do the same along the bottom right of the wing. Wipe the brush and lightly rub to blend.

Lighten the top of the head, the breast and the cheek with Mix 4. Wipe the brush and blend the top of the head to the left and the right, adding a touch of Mix 3 to soften. Take a tiny bit of Mix 4 to join the light area on the head to the back. For the cheek, start at the left corner of the eye and chisel toward the neck with Mix 4. Wipe the brush, add a bit of Mix 3 and blend. Now use the dabber to apply Mix 4 across the breast. Wipe the brush and blend upward and downward. Use touches of Mix 3 to aid in blending.

Load the flat surface of the floral brush with Mix 4. With the paint facing the bird's belly, make elongated C-strokes for wing-feather separations. Let dry.

4 Dampen the red areas, the white belly and the leg puff with gel. Shading of the red on the left side and the rump is done with Animal Black on the dabber, chiseling into the white belly and rump. Wipe the brush and blend away from the white. Then add a line of shading to the red area on the right where it meets the white. Using the floral and True Ochre, lighten the outer edge of the left red area, chiseling toward the wing. Wipe the brush and blend toward the belly.

Using the dabber and Mix 4, chisel shading on the breast toward the black area. Wipe the brush and blend toward the belly. Now apply this shading above and below the branch. Wipe the brush and blend away from the branch on both sides.

Apply a tiny amount of Mix 4 on the leg puff where the leg meets the body. Wipe the brush and blend downward. Side load the liner with Mix 4 and lighten the right edges of the toes. Paint the claws with Mix 3. Let dry.

5 Dampen the tail and black areas with gel. Lighten the white tail-feather tips with Light Buttermilk on a dabber. Start at the tips and work the color upward. Using the floral, further lighten the top of the head, the cheek, the black breast and the top of the beak with Mix 4.

Now dampen the white belly and rump section with gel and deepen the shadows above and below the branch with Mix 4. Lighten the middle of the belly with Light Buttermilk.

Using the liner, add an almond-shaped eye-ring with Mix 4, leaving open corners. Dab a small amount of Burnt Sienna in each corner of the eye. Place a Light Buttermilk highlight at 2 o'clock.

Repaint the beak with Mix 3 and the liner. While Mix 3 remains wet, lighten the top with Mix 4.

Allow the painting to dry completely and then varnish according to the directions on page 9.

II BARN SWALLOW

My friend in England tells me that each spring the barn swallows return to nest in her and her husband's workshops, which are in an old stable. Her husband lets them fly in and build nests just over his head.

I also see these birds each spring. They come to my daughter's barn and busy themselves all day rounding up bits of hay and long hair from the horse's tail. Seeing them weave these hairs into the nest is amazing.

When the fledglings are learning to fly, I enjoy watching them go out together just over the ceiling fan blades. Sometimes the summer breeze blows the blades while the small swallows ride. Then the mother returns to the nest singing, and about five swallows fly back to her. I wonder how they'll all fit back in the nest, but they always seem to manage.

Bird Materials

Paint: Acrylic, DecoArt Americana

Light Buttermilk	Moon Yellow	True Ochre

Burnt Sienna	Baby Blue	Victorian Blue

Animal Black: Burnt Umber + Lamp Black (2:1)	Mix 1: Light Buttermilk + Animal Black (2:1)	Mix 2: Light Buttermilk + Animal Black (3:1)

Surface
• 11" x 14" (27.9cm x 35.6cm) acid-free mounting board

Brushes
Loew-Cornell
• nos. 4 & 8 flats
• no. 1 liner

Nancy Kinney Specialty
• small dabber
• floral

Other
• old scruffy brush for gel retarder
• 2-inch (51mm) wash for varnishing

Additional Supplies
• Jo Sonja's Gel Retarder
• J. W. etc.'s Right-Step Water Base Clear Varnish (Satin)
• paper towels for wiping brush

This pattern may be hand-traced or photocopied for personal use only. Enlarge at 200 percent to bring up to full size.

Background Materials

Paint: Acrylic, DecoArt Americana

Background: Baby Blue

Leaves and branch: Antique Green, Black Green, Baby Blue, Burnt Umber, Light Buttermilk

Brushes
- 2- to 4-inch (51mm to 102mm) sponge roller for basecoating
- no. 8 flat
- small dabber
- no. 1 liner
- old scruffy

Additional Supplies
- 1-inch (25mm) diameter candle with holder
- old stainless steel tablespoon
- Krylon Matte Finish spray 1311
- gel retarder

2 Dip the old scruffy brush into the gel retarder. Wipe the excess on a paper towel and dampen the tail. Use Mix 2 on the chisel edge of the floral to paint the primary wing feather separations in large, irregular V-shaped strokes.

1 Paint the background of your choice as described in chapter 3. I used a twiggy branch with green leaves on a smoked surface.

Transfer the bird pattern.

Most bird basecoating can be done with a no. 8 flat, but if you have trouble in the smaller areas, change to a smaller flat or liner. Chisel the adjoining feather areas into each other as you go (see page 10 for explanation of chiseling). Apply your basecoat colors in this order: Animal Black on the tail, wings, shoulders, head and face mask, leaving a hairline separation between the covert and the secondary wing; Burnt Sienna on the remainder of the body and the eye; Animal Black on the feet; Mix 2 on the beak. While the beak remains wet, load the liner with Mix 1 and separate the top of the beak from the bottom. Let dry.

3 Flat surface double load the floral with Animal Black and Burnt Sienna. With the Burnt Sienna facing the belly area, paint in the secondary-wing feather separations with an elongated C-stroke. Load a small amount of Victorian Blue on the dabber and lighten the back of the secondary wing. Wipe the brush and dab to blend. Let dry.

Barn Swallow, continued

4 Redampen the black portions with gel from the secondary wing up. With Victorian Blue on the dabber, paint C-strokes along the bottom edge of the wing covert. Wipe the brush, load with Animal Black and blend with the Victorian Blue C-strokes that you just painted. This will soften the effect. Still using the dabber, apply Victorian Blue on the shoulders in the middle of the covert and chisel the same color on the neck. Wipe the brush and blend downward. Also place Victorian Blue at the top of the head, wipe the brush and blend forward and backward. Chisel a small amount of the same color at the cheek. If necessary, soften the Victorian Blue with Animal Black. Let dry.

5 Redampen the covert, neck and head with gel. Using Baby Blue on the floral, build up all the Victorian Blue areas to lighten. Soften the Baby Blue with Animal Black if necessary.

6 Dampen all the rust areas with gel. You will now shade with Animal Black on the dabber. Always wipe the brush on a paper towel before blending. Chisel shading into the top of the beak. Blend just a bit. Chisel shading into the beak bottom, moving into the cheek and down the throat. Run shading down the left edge of the body. Also shade under the wing, blending slightly. Side load a no. 4 flat with Animal Black and paint a shadow on the beak where it is attached to the head. Wipe the brush and lightly blend toward the tip of the beak. Let dry.

7 Redampen the bird with gel. Using the floral brush, you will now build the light values on the forehead, above the wing covert and on the belly. Start with a fresh layer of Burnt Sienna, applied lightly. Then apply True Ochre on the wet Burnt Sienna, stroking to blend. Let dry. Apply True Ochre again. Let dry.

Redampen with gel and further lighten with Moon Yellow over the True Ochre. Lighten the top of the beak with Light Buttermilk. Let dry.

8 Paint the eye details with a no. 1 liner. Paint the pupil in Animal Black, leaving edges of the Burnt Sienna showing from 3 o'clock to 5 o'clock on the right edge and from 7 o'clock to 11 o'clock on the left edge. Use Mix 2 for the eye-ring. Add a Light Buttermilk eye sparkle at 11 o'clock.

9 Feet details are also painted with a no. 1 liner. Flatten the liner in Animal Black and side load with Mix 2. With Mix 2 facing left, paint along the left edge of the toes.

Redampen the bird with gel and further build the lights and darks as necessary. Let the painting dry completely and then varnish according to the directions on page 9.

ENGLISH ROBIN

At Christmastime the English Robin's behavior changes. As if he'd caught the holiday spirit, he forgets about territories and searches for a mate. By mid-January most English Robins are paired. The female stops singing, but the male sings every day and well into the night. He's announcing that he's found his mate and, once again, is claiming his territory. Many Christmas cards, especially in England, are adorned with this beautiful robin, which is slightly smaller than the American Robin and quite plump.

Bird Materials

Paint: Acrylic, DecoArt Americana

Light Buttermilk   True Ochre   Georgia Clay

Raw Sienna   Burnt Umber   Animal Black: Burnt Umber + Lamp Black (2:1)

Mix 1: Light Buttermilk + Animal Black (2:1)

Mix 2: Light Buttermilk + Animal Black (3:1)

Mix 6: True Ochre + Georgia Clay (2:1)

Surface
- 11" x 14" (27.9cm x 35.6cm) acid-free mounting board

Brushes
Loew-Cornell
- no. 8 flat
- no. 1 liner

Nancy Kinney Specialty
- small dabber
- floral

Other
- old scruffy brush for gel retarder
- 2-inch (51mm) wash for varnishing

Additional Supplies
- Jo Sonja's Gel Retarder
- J. W. etc.'s Right-Step Water Base Clear Varnish (Satin)
- paper towels for wiping brush

This pattern may be hand-traced or photocopied for personal use only. Enlarge at 222 percent to bring up to full size.

Background Materials

Paint: Acrylic, DecoArt Americana

  Background: Cashmere Beige, Georgia Clay

  Leaves and stems: Antique Green, Black Green, Celery Green

Brushes

- 2- to 4-inch (51mm to 102mm) sponge roller for basecoating
- 1-inch (25mm) wash   • no. 8 flat
- small dabber   • old scruffy

Additional Supplies

- 1-inch (25mm) diameter candle with holder
- old stainless steel tablespoon
- Krylon Matte Finish spray 1311
- gel retarder

1 Paint the background of your choice as described in chapter 3. I used ivy (green leaves) on a smoked surface with Georgia Clay added after the bird was finished. This softens the bird and leaf edges.

    Transfer the bird pattern.

    Most bird basecoating can be done with a no. 8 flat, but if you have trouble in the smaller areas, change to a smaller flat or liner. Chisel the adjoining feather areas into each other as you go (see page 10 for explanation of chiseling). Apply your basecoat colors in this order: Burnt Umber on the tail, back of head and wing; Georgia Clay on the breast; Light Buttermilk on the belly and neck. As you approach the rump with the Light Buttermilk, pick up a small amount of Raw Sienna and chisel back into the belly so the two colors blend while wet. Basecoat the eye, feet and beak in Animal Black. While the beak is still wet, lighten the top of the beak with Mix 2. (Basecoated eye and feet are seen in the next photo.)

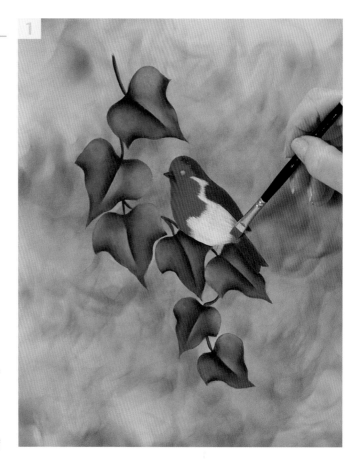

2 Let the bird dry. Then dip an old scruffy brush into the gel retarder. Wipe the excess on a paper towel and dampen the brown areas, which you will shade with Animal Black on the dabber. Remember to wipe your brush before blending. Start with the tail, chiseling into the rump and blending toward the tail tip. Then shade the wing, chiseling into the breast and blending into the wing. Shade the neck and the top of the head, chiseling toward the top of the head and into the rusty part of the head.

    Flat surface double load the floral brush with Animal Black and Mix 1. With Mix 1 facing the belly, make elongated C-strokes to indicate feather separations on the wing and tail. Then load the brush with True Ochre and add small C-stroke feather separations on the wing coverts. Let dry.

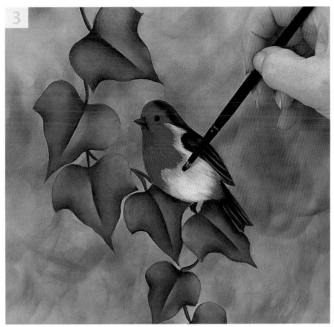

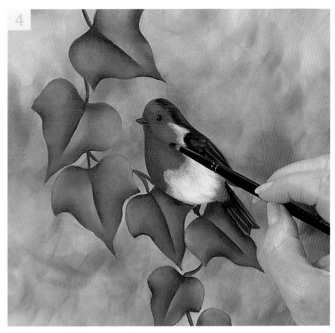

3 Dampen the belly with gel. Load the dabber with Burnt Umber and apply it to the rump tip, chiseling into the Raw Sienna. Now load with Mix 2 and shade the belly, chiseling into the rust area. Wipe the brush and blend into the belly. Let dry.

4 Dampen the rust area with gel. Use the dabber to chisel Burnt Umber into the beak, working back toward the eye area. Apply Burnt Umber under the beak and down the breast. Wipe the brush and blend into the breast. Add a shadow from the beak down into the breast. Wipe the brush and blend. Let dry.

5 Dampen the brown areas with gel. Brush-mix True Ochre + a little Burnt Umber on the dabber and dab a small amount on top of the brown area of the head, working down the head and dabbing on the shoulder to lighten.

Dampen the belly with gel. Load Light Buttermilk on the floral and, using the chisel edge, apply paint to the middle of the belly, chiseling toward the rump and toward the breast.

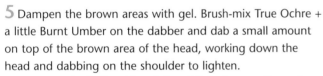

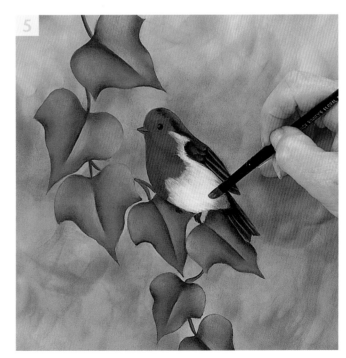

6 Load the floral with Mix 6. Lighten the rust at the top of the head, brushing slightly over the brown. Wipe the brush and chisel toward the beak. Lighten the middle of the jaw, wipe the brush and chisel toward the white and toward the beak. Lighten the middle of the breast. Wipe the brush and chisel toward the belly and toward the beak.

7 Further build the light and dark values as necessary. Paint the eye and feet details with a no. 1 liner. Use Mix 2 for the eye-ring. Paint the pupil with Animal Black, using the liner. Add a Light Buttermilk sparkle at 11 o'clock. Flatten the liner in Animal Black and side load with Mix 2. With Mix 2 facing left, paint along the left edge of the toes.

8 Let the painting dry completely and then varnish according to the directions on page 9.

BALTIMORE ORIOLE

As you might guess, the Baltimore Oriole is the state bird of Maryland. These birds are renowned for their beautiful coloring and flute-like whistle. They build their purse-shaped nest of twigs, milkweed and horse hair to hang from a limb. The male stands guard to stave off predators. After the babies are born, the female brings food to her clamoring, fast-growing nestlings.

Bird Materials

Paint: Acrylic, DecoArt Americana

Light Buttermilk

Cadmium Yellow

Moon Yellow

Burnt Sienna

Animal Black:
Burnt Umber +
Lamp Black (2:1)

Mix 1: Light
Buttermilk +
Animal Black (2:1)

Mix 2: Light
Buttermilk +
Animal Black (3:1)

Surface
• 11" x 14" (27.9cm x 35.6cm) acid-free mounting board

Brushes

Loew-Cornell
• nos. 4 & 8 flats
• no. 1 liner

Nancy Kinney Specialty
• small dabber
• floral

Other
• old scruffy brush for gel retarder
• 2-inch (51mm) wash for varnishing

Additional Supplies
• Jo Sonja's Gel Retarder   • paper towels for wiping brush
• J. W. etc.'s Right-Step Water Base Clear Varnish (Satin)

This pattern may be hand-traced or photocopied for personal use only. Enlarge at 200 percent to bring up to full size.

Background Materials

Paint: Acrylic, DecoArt Americana

Background: Silver Sage Green, Black Green

Leaves and stems: Antique Green, Black Green, Cadmium Yellow, Burnt Sienna

Brushes

- 2- to 4-inch (51mm to 102mm) sponge roller for basecoating
- 1-inch (25mm) wash
- small dabber
- no. 8 flat
- old scruffy

Additional Supplies

- gel retarder

1 Paint the background of your choice as described in chapter 3. I used green leaves on a blended-color surface. Transfer the bird pattern.

Most bird basecoating can be done with a no. 8 flat, but use the no. 1 liner for the beak, eye and wing bar. Chisel the adjoining feather areas into each other as you go (see page 10 for explanation of chiseling). Apply your basecoat colors in this order: Animal Black on the middle tail feathers; Cadmium Yellow on the outside tail feathers; Animal Black on the wing, shoulder, head and eye; Mix 1 on the beak, separating the top and bottom with Animal Black by using the chisel edge of the flat; Light Buttermilk on the wing bar; Cadmium Yellow on the rest of the body. In this photo you see additional eye details, which are explained in step 7. Let dry.

2 Dip an old scruffy brush into the gel retarder. Wipe the excess on a paper towel and dampen the tail with gel. Load the chisel edge of the floral brush in Mix 2 and paint the feather separations on the black tail feathers, curving slightly toward the center. Side load the no. 4 flat with Burnt Sienna and paint a shadow behind the yellow tail feathers. Using the chisel edge of the floral brush and Animal Black, paint thin separation lines on the yellow tail feathers. Let dry.

BALTIMORE ORIOLE, continued

3 Dampen the wings with gel. With Mix 1 on the dabber, shade the upper edge of the white wing bar, chiseling toward the black of the wing. Wipe the brush and put in wing-bar feather separations, using the chisel edge and Mix 1. Apply Mix 1 on the shoulder, wipe the brush and dab up and down to blend. If the Mix 1 is too intense, add Animal Black to aid the blending.

Using Mix 2 on the dabber, paint a very light line on the left side of the shoulder, marking where the secondary wing connects to the wing bar. Using the chisel edge of the floral brush and Mix 2, paint the wing-feather separations in elongated C-strokes. Let dry.

4 Dampen the head with gel. With Mix 2 on the dabber, lighten the top of the head, the cheek area, the back of the neck and the throat. Wipe the brush and dab or lightly rub to blend each area in the direction of feather growth. If the light value is too severe, add Animal Black to aid the blending.

Corner load a no. 4 flat with a bit of Animal Black. With the black facing the head, paint a shadow where the beak is attached to the head. Wipe the brush and lightly blend toward the beak tip. Lighten the beak top with Mix 2.

5 Dampen the yellow area with gel. With the dabber, apply Burnt Sienna along the yellow area just under the neck, chiseling into the black. Wipe the brush and blend downward. Apply Burnt Sienna on the left edge of the yellow breast and belly all the way from the neck to the tail. Wipe the brush and blend into the breast and belly. Apply Burnt Sienna under the left wing. Wipe the brush and blend downward. Let dry.

6 Redampen the yellow area with gel. You will paint the light value using Moon Yellow with the floral brush. Starting on the shoulder above the wing, use the chisel edge of the floral to make a few feather separations over the black wing. Next, lighten the middle of the belly. Wipe the bush and blend up and down. Then lighten the tip of the tail covert, chiseling over the black tail feathers. Let dry.

7 Redampen the bird with gel and further build the light and dark values as necessary. Paint the eye and feet details with a no. 1 liner. Use Mix 2 for the eye-ring. Add a Light Buttermilk sparkle at 10 o'clock. Base in the feet with Animal Black. While this color remains wet, lighten the edges of the toes with Mix 2.

Let the painting dry completely and then varnish according to the directions on page 9.

Project 14 *A*MERICAN ROBIN

What would we do without the ordinary American robin? There's hardly a time of the day you can't glance into your yard and see them scratching for earthworms or insects–their main diet. And just as I've been writing this paragraph, a robin has hopped to my birdbath for a drink of fresh water. He dips his head in and then holds it high to let the cool liquid refresh his throat. Watching him makes the effort of providing water for birds worthwhile.

The robin is a devoted parent, building a sturdy nest from twigs and mud and lining it with soft material. Each nest will hold three to four blue eggs.

Bird Materials

Paint: Acrylic, DecoArt Americana

Light Buttermilk

Cadmium Yellow

Moon Yellow

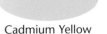

True Ochre

Fawn

Burnt Sienna

Burnt Umber

Animal Black: Burnt Umber + Lamp Black (2:1)

Mix 1: Light Buttermilk + Animal Black (2:1)

Mix 2: Light Buttermilk + Animal Black (3:1)

Surface
• 11" x 14" (27.9cm x 35.6cm) acid-free mounting board

Brushes
Loew-Cornell
• nos. 4 & 8 flats
• no. 1 liner

Nancy Kinney Specialty
• small dabber
• floral

Other
• old scruffy brush for gel retarder
• 2-inch (51mm) wash for varnishing

Additional Supplies
• Jo Sonja's Gel Retarder   • paper towels for wiping brush
• J. W. etc.'s Right-Step Water Base Clear Varnish (Satin)

This pattern may be hand-traced or photocopied for personal use only. Enlarge at 193 percent to bring up to full size.

Background Materials

Paint: Acrylic, DecoArt Americana

Background: Driftwood, Arbor Green

Branch and nest: Animal Black (See bird colors.), Burnt Umber, Burnt Sienna, Moon Yellow, Raw Sienna, True Ochre, Arbor Green, Fawn

Brushes
- 2- to 4-inch (51mm to 102mm) sponge roller for basecoating
- no. 8 flat
- floral
- no. 1 liner
- old scruffy

Additional Supplies
- plastic wrap
- spray mist water bottle
- large sea sponge
- gel retarder

1 Paint the background of your choice as described in chapter 3. I used a birch branch with a nest on a sponge-and-plastic wrap surface. Transfer the pattern.

Most basecoating of the bird can be done with a no. 8 flat, but if you have trouble in the smaller areas, change to a smaller flat or liner. Chisel the adjoining feather areas into each other as you go (see page 10 for explanation of chiseling). Apply your basecoat colors in this order: Burnt Umber on the tail, wing, covert, neck and head; Light Buttermilk on the rump and the eye stripes; Burnt Sienna on the breast and belly; Cadmium Yellow on the beak; Animal Black on the eye.

2 Let the bird dry. Then dip an old scruffy brush into the gel retarder. Wipe the excess on a paper towel and dampen the tail and wings. Using Animal Black on the dabber, shade at the base of the tail, chiseling into the white rump. Wipe the brush and blend down toward the tail tip.

Separate the two wings with Animal Black on the chisel edge of the dabber, working all the way from the wing tip to the neck and then continuing under the cheek bone and up the side of the head. Chisel shading on the foreground wing into the breast and also into the wing covert. Wipe and blend both shaded areas down toward the tip of the wing.

AMERICAN ROBIN, continued

3 Dampen the head and beak with gel. Using the dabber and Animal Black, chisel shading into the beak and paint the color around the entire eye and under the throat. Wipe the brush and blend.

Side load a no. 4 flat with Burnt Sienna. Apply the color at the back of the beak where the beak is attached to the head. Chisel the Burnt Sienna towards the tip of the beak. Wipe the brush often on a paper towel. Turn the brush over and put a dab of Burnt Sienna at the beak tip, working back slightly to blend. Let dry. Redampen the beak and reinforce the shading with Burnt Umber at the head. Separate the top and bottom of the beak with Burnt Umber on the chisel edge of a no. 4 flat. Let dry.

4 Redampen the brown areas with gel. Using the dabber, pull Burnt Sienna forward from the tail tip toward the body. Also lighten the top of the front wing and the wing covert's edge. While the Burnt Sienna is still wet, further lighten the top of the front wing with Fawn. Wipe the brush and blend. Do the same with the wing covert edge.

Flat surface double load the floral in Fawn and Animal Black. Using the chisel edge of the brush, pull elongated C-strokes for wing feather separations. Using the no. 4 flat side-loaded in Fawn, paint small C-strokes on top of the feather separations. Let dry.

5 Dampen the head with gel. Lighten the crown with Fawn, using the chisel edge of the floral. Wipe the brush and blend forward and backward. Side load the floral with Fawn and chisel the light value into the cheek area (visible in the next photo). Paint throat speckles with a no. 4 flat corner-loaded with Fawn. Using the liner, paint in the tiny light areas just above and below the eye. Let dry.

6 Dampen the rust area and the rump with gel. Using Mix 1 on the dabber, chisel shading on the rump back into the rust area. Wipe the brush and blend out into the rump. Using Animal Black on the dabber, chisel under the neck and continue brushing down the breast and on the outside edge of the body just behind the nest. Also shade under the neck and the wing. Wipe the brush and blend the shading into the body.

7 While the breast and belly are wet, add a thin, fresh layer of Burnt Sienna. Begin adding light value with True Ochre while the Burnt Sienna remains wet. Let dry. Redampen with gel and further lighten the breast with Moon Yellow. Lighten the top of the beak with Moon Yellow, using the chisel edge of a no. 4 flat. Let dry.

8 Redampen the bird with gel and further build the lights and darks as necessary. Paint the eye details with a no. 1 liner. Use Mix 2 for the eye-ring. Add a Light Buttermilk sparkle at 10 o'clock.

Let the painting dry completely and then varnish according to the directions on page 9.

NORTHERN CARDINAL

The cardinal is special to me. He constantly perches outside my window to eat from the bird feeder, and it amazes me that he never fails to carry sunflower seed down to his mate who waits patiently on the ground. He then cracks the sunflower seed for her. This cardinal is definitely not into women's lib! In fact, the male cardinal is a devoted mate and may have up to three broods in one season. The young nestlings will fly down with the parents and eat alongside them, and the father cardinal will also crack their seeds.

The cardinal is the state bird of Illinois, North Carolina, Ohio, Kentucky, Indiana, West Virginia and Virginia—quite a popular bird!

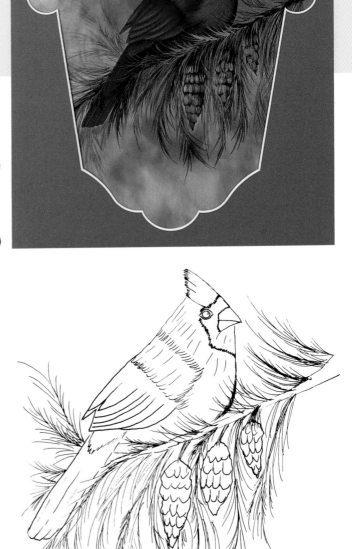

Bird Materials

Paint: Acrylic, DecoArt Americana

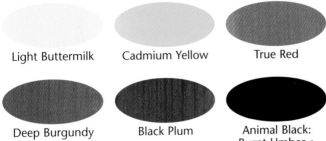

Light Buttermilk   Cadmium Yellow   True Red

Deep Burgundy   Black Plum   Animal Black:
Burnt Umber +
Lamp Black (2:1)

Surface
• 11" x 14" (27.9cm x 35.6cm) acid-free mounting board

Brushes
Loew-Cornell
• no. 8 flat
• no. 1 liner

Nancy Kinney Specialty
• small dabber
• floral

Other
• old scruffy brush for gel retarder
• 2-inch (51mm) wash for varnishing

Additional Supplies
• Jo Sonja's Gel Retarder   • paper towels for wiping brush
• J. W. etc.'s Right-Step Water Base Clear Varnish (Satin)

This pattern may be hand-traced or photocopied for personal use only. Enlarge at 222 percent to bring up to full size.

Background Materials

Paint: Acrylic, DecoArt Americana

   Background: Driftwood, Black Green, Deep Burgundy

   Pine branch: Burnt Umber, Animal Black (See bird colors.), Black Green, Celery Green

   Cones: Burnt Umber, Animal Black (See bird colors.), Burnt Sienna, True Ochre, Moon Yellow

Brushes

- 2- to 4-inch (51mm to 102mm) sponge roller for basecoating
- 1-inch (25mm) wash
- floral
- no. 8 flat
- old scruffy

Additional Supplies

- 1-inch (25mm) diameter candle with holder
- old stainless steel tablespoon
- Krylon Matte Finish spray 1311
- gel retarder

1 Paint the background of your choice as described in chapter 3. I used a pine branch with cones on a smoked surface with added washes of color. Transfer the bird pattern.

   Most bird basecoating can be done with a no. 8 flat, but if you have trouble in the smaller areas, change to a smaller flat or liner. Chisel the adjoining feather areas into each other as you go (see page 10 for explanation of chiseling). Apply your basecoat colors in this order: Deep Burgundy everywhere except the eye, mask and beak; True Red on the beak; Animal Black on the mask and eye. As you base in these areas, notice that I have left a fine pattern line showing between the different areas of the bird. You can see this especially well around the eye.

2 Let the bird dry. Then dip an old scruffy brush into the gel retarder. Blot the excess on a paper towel and then dampen the entire bird. For the rest of this step, you will use Black Plum as a shading value on the dabber. Chisel shading in the following order of body parts, wiping the brush and blending each application:

   a. under the wing on the tail covert

   b. under the wing covert, chiseling into the wing covert

   c. under the neck, chiseling into the neck and down the side

   d. under the crown to the eye

   e. into the mask area and continuing, without chiseling, down the front of the bird

   f. the lower edge of the body, above the branch

   g. under the wing

   h. on the crown above the mask, brushing upward

   i. on the tip of the crest, brushing toward the beak

   j. at the base of the beak, brushing toward the head.

Let dry.

3 Flat surface double load the floral brush with Black Plum and True Red. With True Red facing the belly, use the chisel edge to paint wing separations in elongated C-strokes. Then, using the same technique, paint the tail-feather separations. Let dry.

4 Dampen the bird with gel. Using the dabber, apply Black Plum to further build shading depth in the areas you painted in step 2. Also strengthen the tail-feather separations using a flat surface double-loaded floral with Black Plum and True Red.

5 While the bird is still damp, you will chisel in the light value, using True Red on the floral. Paint in the following order of body parts, wiping the brush and blending after each application:

    a. on the back and over the wing, blending toward the head

    b. on the neck, blending toward the eye

    c. in the middle of the head, chiseling toward the beak and the crown tip

    d. on the edges of the tail covert, blending toward the wing.

Then brush True Red on the belly front, stroking with the body contour and feather growth. Let dry.

6 Redampen the entire bird with gel. Brush-mix True Red + Cadmium Yellow on the floral. Chisel in a touch of this color in the lighter red areas of the wing and tail coverts. Lighten the back area, chiseling over the wing. Wipe the brush and blend toward the neck. Lighten the neck area, wipe the brush and blend toward the eye. Lighten the breast, chiseling over the wing. Lighten the middle of the crown, wipe the brush and chisel toward the crown tip and the beak. Dab a small amount of light value at the top of the beak, wipe the brush and pat to blend.

7 Paint the eye details with a no. 1 liner. Use True Red to paint the eye-ring. Flatten the liner in Animal Black and side load with a tiny amount of Light Buttermilk. Then paint a C-stroke from 11 o'clock to 7 o'clock. Add a Light Buttermilk sparkle at 2 o'clock.

8 Let the painting dry, redampen with gel, and further build the lights and darks as necessary. Let the painting dry completely and then varnish according to the directions on page 9.

NORTHERN MOCKINGBIRD

Perhaps you remember the song, "Listen to the Mocking-bird." This bird can sing for hours and has the ability to mimic many other birds' calls. Just the other day, I looked up to what I thought was going to be a chickadee; instead, it was a large gray mockingbird. I know he was thinking, *I fooled you—you looked.*

The mockingbird is a common songbird found across North America. It's the state bird of Arkansas, Florida, Mississippi and Texas.

Bird Materials

Paint: Acrylic, DecoArt Americana

Light Buttermilk

Burnt Umber

Animal Black: Burnt Umber + Lamp Black (2:1)

Mix 1: Light Buttermilk + Animal Black (2:1)

Mix 2: Light Buttermilk + Animal Black (3:1)

Surface
• 11" x 14" (27.9cm x 35.6cm) acid-free mounting board

Brushes
Loew-Cornell
• nos. 4, 6 & 8 flats
• no. 1 liner

Nancy Kinney Specialty
• small dabber
• floral

Other
• old scruffy brush for gel retarder
• 2-inch (51mm) wash for varnishing

Additional Supplies
• Jo Sonja's Gel Retarder   • paper towels for wiping brush
• J. W. etc.'s Right-Step Water Base Clear Varnish (Satin)

Background Materials

Paint: Acrylic, DecoArt Americana
Background: Celery Green

Hydrangea and leaves: Dioxazine Purple, Light Buttermilk, Antique Green, Black Green, True Ochre, Celery Green

Brushes
• 2- to 4-inch (51mm to 102mm) sponge roller for basecoating
• no. 8 flat   • small dabber   • floral
• no. 1 liner   • old scruffy

Additional Supplies
• 1-inch (25mm) diameter candle with holder
• old stainless steel tablespoon
• Krylon Matte Finish spray 1311   • gel retarder

This pattern may be hand-traced or photocopied for personal use only. Enlarge at 222 percent to bring up to full size.

1 Paint the background of your choice as described in chapter 3. I used a hydrangea with green leaves on a smoked surface. Transfer the bird pattern.

Most bird basecoating can be done with a no. 8 flat, but if you have trouble in the smaller areas, change to a smaller flat or liner. Chisel the adjoining feather areas into each other as you go (see page 10 for explanation of chiseling). Apply your basecoat colors in this order: Mix 1 on the tail, beak and wings; Mix 2 on the belly, breast, back and neck. As you work toward the top of the head with Mix 2, gradually pick up Mix 1, blending the two colors as you go. Base the eye in Animal Black. With a no. 1 liner, add C-strokes of Burnt Umber on each side of the black pupil.

2 Let the bird dry. Then dip an old scruffy brush into the gel retarder. Wipe the excess on a paper towel and dampen the entire bird. With Animal Black on the dabber, shade where the tail comes out from under the flower. Wipe the brush and blend toward the tail tip. Chisel shading on the wing into the shoulder. Wipe the brush and blend down into the wing.

Side load a no. 6 flat with Animal Black and paint a shadow where the beak is attached to the head. Chisel slightly back toward the head, wipe the brush and blend toward the beak tip. Using the chisel edge of the brush, add a line of Animal Black to separate the beak top and bottom.

With the dabber, chisel Animal Black from the beak up around the eye and down the side of the head. Wipe the brush and lightly chisel toward the back of the head.

With Mix 1 on the dabber, add belly shading under the wing and above the flower and behind the leaf. Wipe the brush and blend up into the belly. Using Animal Black, paint a shadow under the beak and down the left side of the neck. Chisel irregular strokes of Mix 1 along the cheek line. Wipe the brush and blend down into the neck.

3 Flat surface double load the floral with Animal Black and Mix 2. With Mix 2 facing the belly, swing in the elongated tail and wing feather separation strokes. Side load the no. 4 flat and stagger two rows of tiny C-stroke feather separations on the upper wing.

With Mix 2 on the floral, lighten the top of the beak. Wipe the brush and pat to blend. With Light Buttermilk on the floral, lighten the top of the head, chiseling toward the beak and the back of the head. Chisel Light Buttermilk on the cheek. Wipe the brush and blend lightly toward the beak. Lighten the breast by chiseling Light Buttermilk over the wing and in long curved strokes that work their way across the breast toward the right side of the body. Wipe the brush and blend upward and downward.

4 (See photo of completed bird on page 84.) After the bird dries, redampen with gel retarder and strengthen the lights and the darks as needed. Use the same light and dark values as called for in the above instructions. Use the no. 1 liner for eye details. Paint the eye-ring with Mix 2. Add a Light Buttermilk sparkle at 10 o'clock. Let the painting dry completely and then varnish according to the directions on page 9.

SCISSOR-TAILED FLYCATCHER

The scissor-tailed flycatcher spends most of the summer in the southern United States, migrating to Mexico and Central America in the winter. Birders send me good photos and I marvel at its beauty, although I've never been privileged to see the real thing. The adult is fairly large with a magnificent forked tail. In fact, I recently noticed that in all my photos, the flycatcher's tail is as long as his body.

Bird Materials

Paint: Acrylic, DecoArt Americana

Light Buttermilk

Shading Flesh

True Red

Deep Burgundy

Black Plum

Animal Black:
Burnt Umber +
Lamp Black (2:1)

Mix 1: Light
Buttermilk +
Animal Black (2:1)

Mix 2: Light
Buttermilk +
Animal Black (3:1)

Surface
- 11" x 14" (27.9cm x 35.6cm) acid-free mounting board

Brushes
Loew-Cornell
- nos. 4 & 8 flats
- no. 1 liner

Nancy Kinney Specialty
- small dabber
- floral

Other
- old scruffy brush for gel retarder
- 2-inch (51mm) wash for varnishing

Additional Supplies
- Jo Sonja's Gel Retarder
- J. W. etc.'s Right-Step Water Base Clear Varnish (Satin)
- paper towels for wiping brush

This pattern may be hand-traced or photocopied for personal use only. Enlarge at 200 percent to bring up to full size.

Background Materials

Paint: Acrylic, DecoArt Americana

Background: Arbor Green, Light Buttermilk, Black Green

Hydrangea and stems: Arbor Green, Deep Burgundy, True Red, Shading Flesh, Celery Green, Plantation Pine

Brushes
- 2- to 4-inch (51mm to 102mm) sponge roller for basecoating
- no. 8 flat
- no. 1 liner
- old scruffy
- floral

Additional Supplies
- gel retarder

1 Paint the background of your choice as described in chapter 3. I used a hydrangea on a multi-colored rolled surface. Transfer the bird pattern.

When basecoating the bird, chisel the adjoining feather areas into each other as you go (see page 10 for explanation of chiseling). For the beak, use Mix 1 on a no. 1 liner, lightening the beak top with Mix 2 while it's still wet. Add a tiny amount of Animal Black where the beak is attached to the head, lightly blending toward the beak tip. Base the crown with Deep Burgundy using a no. 4 flat, chiseling down into the head. Base the wing side bar with Deep Burgundy on the no. 1 liner, chiseling into the wing and into the breast areas. Paint the outer tail edges with Light Buttermilk and a no. 1 liner. Complete the rest of the basecoating with a no. 8 flat, remembering to chisel adjoining feather areas into each other. Proceed in the following order: Animal Black on the inner tail feathers; Mix 1 on the tail covert and primary wings; Mix 2 on the wing coverts and the remainder of the body; Animal Black on the eye. Then load the floral in Animal Black and side load with Light Buttermilk for a series of long comma-like strokes along the inside edges of the tail feathers.

2 Let the bird dry. Then dip an old scruffy brush into the gel retarder. Wipe the excess on a paper towel and dampen the tail, tail covert and primary wings. With the dabber, apply Animal Black shading on the tail covert under the wings. Wipe the brush and blend toward the covert tip. Then shade the white tail feathers, painting this shading color along the outside edges of the dark tail feathers. Leave a bit of unshaded Light Buttermilk on the outside edges of the white tail feathers.

3 Dampen the wings and the top of the head with gel. With Animal Black on the dabber, shade up the right side of the left wing to separate the wings. Shade under the bottom edges of the wing coverts, chiseling up. Wipe the brush and blend down the wings. Also shade the left edge of the left wing, chiseling into the belly area.

Indicate a few Animal Black feathers on the wing coverts by making jagged V-shaped strokes with the chisel edge of the dabber. Use Mix 1 to shade the V-shaped area above and between the wing coverts. Start near the red wing bar and work down into the V and then up again to the outside. Wipe the brush and blend.

Use Black Plum on the dabber to shade the red crown, chiseling down into the head. Also add a shadow on the left of the red wing bar, chiseling toward the breast.

4 With Mix 1 on the dabber, chisel into the beak, completely around the eye, under the beak and down the front of the throat. To create the cheek line, chisel Mix 1 in a curve from the throat toward the back of the head. Wipe the brush and blend downward. Add Mix 1 shading on the belly area beside the flower and tail. Wipe the brush and blend up toward the belly.

5 Flat surface double load the floral with Animal Black and Mix 2. With Mix 2 facing the body, make elongated C-strokes down the left wing to indicate feather separations. Then add feather separations in the shape of thick Vs on the right wing.

Dampen the head and breast with gel. Load Light Buttermilk on the floral for the light value. Start in the middle of the breast and brush up and down, chiseling over the red wing bar. Lighten the gray portion of the top of the head, chiseling into the crown and working down the back of the head. Wipe the brush and blend. Lighten the neck and the cheek with the chisel edge of the floral.

6 With the chisel edge of the floral, take a small amount of Shading Flesh and brush into the belly area to create a reflection of the flower's color. Then load the floral with True Red, side loading in Shading Flesh. Chisel in the top edge of the red crown. Lighten the right edge of the red wing bar in the same manner.

7 Further build the lights and darks as necessary. Paint the eye details with a no. 1 liner. Use Mix 2 for the eye-ring. Add a Light Buttermilk sparkle at 11 o'clock.

Let the painting dry completely and then varnish according to the directions on page 9.

ℬLUE TIT

A British woman writing about blue tits in her garden mentioned that one morning she saw a family party of nine. They thoroughly examined each twig and leaf for insects and spiders—just the right breakfast.

The blue tit is one of the most common birds in Britain, but I look at all its beautiful colors and am amazed that anyone would think of the bird as common.

I've heard of blue tits tearing open the foil tops of milk bottles and drinking the top layer of cream. Groups of these birds have even been known to follow milkmen or wait for milk deliveries. That milk would come in handy in the winter when all the insects are gone.

Bird Materials

Paint: Acrylic, DecoArt Americana

Light Buttermilk	Moon Yellow	Antique Green
Black Green	Baby Blue	Victorian Blue
Prussian Blue	Raw Sienna	Burnt Sienna
Animal Black: Burnt Umber + Lamp Black (2:1)	Mix 1: Light Buttermilk + Animal Black (2:1)	Mix 2: Light Buttermilk + Animal Black (3:1)

Surface
• 11" x 14" (27.9cm x 35.6cm) acid-free mounting board

Brushes
Loew-Cornell
• nos. 4 & 8 flats
• no. 1 liner

Nancy Kinney Specialty
• small dabber
• floral

Other
• old scruffy brush for gel retarder
• 2-inch (51mm) wash for varnishing

Additional Supplies
• Jo Sonja's Gel Retarder   • paper towels for wiping brush
• J. W. etc.'s Right-Step Water Base Clear Varnish (Satin)

This pattern may be hand-traced or photocopied for personal use only. Enlarge at 222 percent to bring up to full size.

Background Materials

Paint: Acrylic, DecoArt Americana

 Background: Grey Sky

 Pussy willow branch: Burnt Umber, Light Buttermilk, Black Green, Raw Sienna, True Ochre

Brushes

- 2- to 4-inch (51mm to 102mm) sponge roller for basecoating
- no. 8 flat
- no. 1 liner
- small dabber
- old scruffy

Additional Supplies

- 1-inch (25mm) diameter candle with holder
- old stainless steel tablespoon
- Krylon Matte Finish spray 1311
- gel retarder

1 Paint the background of your choice as described in chapter 3. I used a twiggy branch with pussy willows on a smoked surface. Transfer the bird pattern.

Most bird basecoating can be done with a no. 8 flat, but if you have trouble in the smaller areas, change to a smaller flat or liner. Chisel the adjoining feather areas into each other as you go (see page 10 for explanation of chiseling). Apply your basecoat colors in this order: Victorian Blue on the tail, wing and top of the head; Antique Green on the wing coverts; Animal Black on the mask and neck; Light Buttermilk on the remainder of the face and neck; Moon Yellow on the breast, belly and rump; Mix 1 on the beak and feet. Leave a hairline space between your blue colors so that you will not lose your pattern. Let dry.

2 Dip an old scruffy brush into the gel retarder. Wipe the excess on a paper towel and dampen the blue areas. In this step you will be shading with Prussian Blue, using the dabber. Always wipe the brush before you blend. Shade along the back under the wings, and then blend down the back. Use the chisel edge to darken between the two tail sections. Chisel shading on the wings into the green wing coverts. Blend down the wings and back. Separate the feather edges on the back wing. Shade the primary wing to separate the two secondary wings. Now separate the feathers on the foreground primary wing. Then shade the crown by chiseling color into the white of the head. Wipe the brush and blend toward the top of the head. Separate the two tail feathers with Prussian Blue. Wipe the brush and lightly blend the harsh edge.

BLUE TIT, continued

3 Basecoat the eye in Animal Black. Let dry and dampen the green wing coverts and the head with gel. Now you will shade these areas. Remember to wipe the brush before blending. Side load the floral in Black Green and chisel shading on the green coverts into the black neckband and the yellow breast. Blend toward the wing. Again, side load Black Green on the floral and, with the paint side of the brush up, paint small jagged feather separations on the coverts.

For the white facial areas, use Mix 2 on a floral. Start shading at the beak, moving up the head and around the top of the eye. Also shade under the eye and down the right of the black throat area. Then, in the white area to the left of the black throat area, shade under the beak and down the throat. Further shade the very outside edge of this area with Mix 1.

Corner load the no. 4 flat with Animal Black and paint a shadow where the beak is attached to the head. Lightly blend this color down toward the tip of the beak. Use the chisel edge to separate the beak top and bottom with Animal Black.

4 Dampen the yellow area with gel. With Raw Sienna on the dabber, shade under the black neckband, chiseling up into the black area. Wipe the brush and blend downward into the breast. Shade the outer edges of the breast and belly as well as under the wing. Wipe the brush and blend into the yellow areas. Tip the dabber in Raw Sienna and make light staggered V-shaped feather markings. Let dry.

5 Deepen the shading on the yellow areas and on the V shapes with Burnt Sienna on the dabber.

6 To begin adding light values, dampen the blue areas with gel. Load one side of the floral with Baby Blue. Using the chisel edge, paint tail feather separations and feather edges on the back wing. Flat surface double load the floral with Prussian Blue and Baby Blue. Keeping the Baby Blue toward the bird's body, pull elongated feather separations on the front primary wing. Side load the floral with Baby Blue and paint C-stroke separations on the secondary wings. Use the floral to lighten the very top of the head with Baby Blue. Let dry.

7 Dampen the head, breast and beak with gel. With Light Buttermilk on the floral, lighten the top of the white face area and the bottom of the white jaw area, chiseling into the surrounding feathers. Wipe the brush and blend toward the middle of the face. Lighten the top of the beak with the same color. Add light value to the breast with Moon Yellow, chiseling over the green covert. Further lighten the middle of the breast and belly, working between the feather markings. Let dry.

8 Redampen the bird with gel and further build the lights and darks as necessary. Paint the eye details with a no. 1 liner. Use Mix 2 for the eye-ring. Add a Light Buttermilk sparkle at 11 o'clock. Let the painting dry completely and then varnish according to the directions on page 9.

The European greenfinch is a large bird that has invaded the gardens of Europe over the last century. Their big conical bills can crack large seeds efficiently, and they're particularly fond of sunflower seeds. The song they sing is considered dull, described by some as very nasal. I say their beauty makes up for whatever their singing lacks.

Bird Materials

Paint: Acrylic, DecoArt Americana

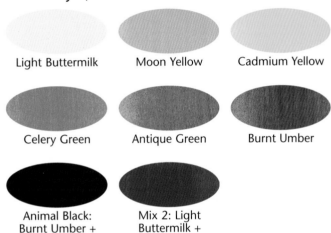

Light Buttermilk   Moon Yellow   Cadmium Yellow

Celery Green   Antique Green   Burnt Umber

Animal Black: Burnt Umber + Lamp Black (2:1)

Mix 2: Light Buttermilk + Animal Black (3:1)

Surface
• 11" x 14" (27.9cm x 35.6cm) acid-free mounting board

Brushes
Loew-Cornell
• nos. 4 & 8 flats
• no. 1 liner

Nancy Kinney Specialty
• small dabber

Other
• old scruffy brush for gel retarder
• 2-inch (51mm) wash for varnishing

Additional Supplies
• Jo Sonja's Gel Retarder
• J. W. etc.'s Right-Step Water Base Clear Varnish (Satin)
• paper towels for wiping brush

This pattern may be hand-traced or photocopied for personal use only. Enlarge at 182 percent to bring up to full size.

Background Materials

Paint: Acrylic, DecoArt Americana
  Background: Driftwood
  Branch: Mix 1 (See page 6.), Mix 2 (See bird colors.)

Brushes
- 2- to 4-inch (51mm to 102mm) sponge roller for basecoating
- no. 8 flat
- no. 1 liner
- old scruffy

Additional Supplies
- gel retarder

1 Paint the background of your choice as described in chapter 3. I used a twiggy branch on a rolled surface. Transfer the bird pattern.

Most bird basecoating can be done with a no. 8 flat, but if you have trouble in the smaller areas, change to a smaller flat or liner. Chisel the adjoining feather areas into each other as you go (see page 10 for explanation of chiseling). Apply your basecoat colors in this order: Animal Black on the inner tail feathers; Cadmium Yellow on the outer tail feathers; Animal Black on the large upper part of the end portion of the wing; Cadmium Yellow on the lower edge of the end portion of the wing; Antique Green on the body and head; Moon Yellow on the beak; Animal Black on the eyes and feet. Let dry.

2 Dip an old scruffy brush into the gel retarder. Wipe the excess on a paper towel and dampen the tail and wing. Double load a no. 4 flat in Animal Black and Cadmium Yellow. Start at the tip of the right black tail feather and slide up the middle of the tail to separate. Repeat this technique on all the black tail feathers to indicate gathered tail feather edges. Load the chisel edge of a no. 4 flat with Animal Black and pull up the tail to separate the black tail feathers from the yellow tail feather edges. Paint wing-feather separation lines in the same manner and with the same colors as you did for the tail. Remember to separate the yellow wing feather edges with strokes of Animal Black.

EUROPEAN GREENFINCH, continued

3 Dampen the upper half of the bird with gel. Using Animal Black on the dabber, paint a shadow by chiseling on the wing into the shoulder and down the left side. Wipe the brush and blend into the wing. Add a shoulder separation line, as you see me doing in this photo.

4 With Animal Black on the dabber, chisel shading on the face into the beak. Wipe the brush and pull the color back around the eye. Wipe the brush and blend into the face and throat. Add shading on the breast under the throat. Wipe the brush and blend into the breast. Shade under the wing and into the rump. Then shade down the left edge of the body. Wipe the brush and blend all three areas to soften. Let dry.

5 Dampen the beak with gel. Side load a no. 4 flat with Burnt Umber. Paint Burnt Umber where the beak is attached to the head. Wipe the brush and blend toward the beak tip. Separate the top and bottom of the beak with the chisel edge of the brush, using Burnt Umber. Lighten the top beak tip with Light Buttermilk. Wipe the brush and pat to blend.

6 Make sure the bird is dry and then redampen the green areas with gel. With the dabber, apply Celery Green to the wing covert, chiseling over the black wing. Wipe the brush and blend back up into the covert. Using the chisel edge, make staggered C-shaped feather separations with Celery Green.

7 The light value in this step is done with Celery Green on the dabber. Always wipe the brush before blending. Lighten the top of the head and blend to the right and to the left. Lighten under the eye and again blend to the right and to the left. Lighten the neck, chiseling downward and blending upward. Lighten the breast, chiseling over the shoulder and blending toward the rump and toward the neck. Let dry.

8 Further build the lights and darks as necessary. Paint the eye and feet details with a no. 1 liner. Use Mix 2 for the eye-ring. Add a Light Buttermilk sparkle at 11 o'clock. Load the brush with Light Buttermilk and paint a C-stroke from 3 o'clock to 5 o'clock to indicate the pupil. To paint the toes, load the no. 1 liner in Animal Black, side loading with Mix 2. Paint the claws with Animal Black.

Let the painting dry completely and then varnish according to the directions on page 9.

The blue jay, a widespread bird related to the crow, sings many different songs and can sound like other birds. He's almost turquoise as the sun reflects across his back.

Jays often get a bad rap. Most people think of them as aggressive, but basically they're just noisy. They sit on limbs, watching other birds eat from the feeder, waiting patiently for a turn at those good seeds. Recently I saw a black-capped chickadee run a blue jay from the feeder. The tiny chickadee flew at the large bird, which just fluttered away. Could that jay have thought that maybe the little guy needed the food more than he did?

Bird Materials

Paint: Acrylic, DecoArt Americana

Light Buttermilk

Moon Yellow

Baby Blue

Victorian Blue

Prussian Blue

Dioxazine Purple

Animal Black:
Burnt Umber +
Lamp Black (2:1)

Mix 1: Light
Buttermilk +
Animal Black (2:1)

Mix 2: Light
Buttermilk +
Animal Black (3:1)

Surface
• wood scalloped heart plate, 11½" x 11½" (29.2cm x 29.2cm) available from The Artist's Club (See Resources, page 126.)

Brushes
Loew-Cornell
• nos. 8 & 12 flats
• no. 1 liner

Nancy Kinney Specialty
• small dabber
• floral

Other
• old scruffy brush for gel retarder
• 2-inch (51mm) wash for varnishing

Additional Supplies
• Jo Sonja's Gel Retarder • paper towels for wiping brush
• J. W. etc.'s Right-Step Water Base Clear Varnish (Satin)

This pattern may be hand-traced or photocopied for personal use only. Enlarge at 172 percent to bring up to full size.

Background Materials

Paint: Acrylic, DecoArt Americana

    Background: Arbor Green, Black Forest Green, Victorian Blue, Light Buttermilk

    Pine branch: Black Green, Hauser Medium Green, Victorian Blue, Light Buttermilk

Brushes

- 2- to 4-inch (51mm to 102mm) sponge roller for basecoating,
- 1-inch (25mm) wash
- floral
- no. 8 flat
- old scruffy

Additional Supplies

- gel retarder

1 Paint the background of your choice as described in chapter 3. I used pine branches on a blended-color surface. The branches in the border are drawn freehand. Transfer the bird pattern.

Most bird basecoating can be done with a no. 8 flat, but if you have trouble in the smaller areas, change to a smaller flat or liner. Chisel the adjoining feather areas into each other as you go (see page 10 for explanation of chiseling). Apply your basecoat colors in this order: Light Buttermilk on the outside tail feathers, rump, belly, breast, throat and eyebrow; Victorian Blue on the tail, wings, back and crest (feathers above the head); Mix 1 on the beak; Animal Black on the feet, eye, neckband and face stripe. Let dry.

2 Dip an old scruffy brush into the gel retarder. Wipe the excess on a paper towel and dampen the tail. Using the dabber with Prussian Blue, shade the tail under the wing without chiseling. Wipe the brush and blend down the tail. With Mix 1, shade the inside edge of the white tail feathers. With a no. 1 liner and Animal Black, separate the tail down the middle with a thin line. Then paint the black C-shaped bars, chiseling the tops and bottoms of each bar.

3 With Animal Black still on your liner, paint feather separations parallel to the line down the middle of the tail. While this area remains damp from the gel retarder, lighten between the black lines with a brush mix of Victorian Blue + Baby Blue on the liner. Let dry.

4 Dampen the wings with gel. Load the dabber with Prussian Blue and separate the wings by placing a shadow on the back wing. Continue your shading above the wing at the shoulder and under the black neckband. Wipe the brush and blend. Shade in the middle of the foreground wing, blending back and forth. Shade the upper end of the foreground wing, chiseling into the breast.

5 Using the no. 1 liner, paint two black wing bars (appearing as a series of C-shaped strokes) on the upper portion of the foreground wing with Animal Black. Then paint the white wing bars in Light Buttermilk. Next add a final black wing bar, chiseling into the bottom of the white wing bar. Indicate a few wing bar separations on the background wing as you see in the photo. Then return to the foreground wing and separate the white wing bar C-shapes with Animal Black.

6 Flat surface double load the floral with Baby Blue and Prussian Blue. With Baby Blue toward the belly, paint feather separations in long Vs on the bottom half of the foreground wing. Then using a liner with Animal Black, chisel in black feather bars on the lower half of the foreground wing. Let dry.

7 Dampen the white areas with gel. You will now shade with Mix 1 on the dabber. Shade the breast and belly under the wing, working back toward the rump. Wipe the brush and lightly blend. Separate the rump from the belly with a bit of shading. Blend toward the tail. Shade the right outside edge of the body from the rump to the black neckband. Blend into the belly of the bird. Chisel shading across the breast under the black neckband. Wipe the brush and blend toward the belly. Chisel shading into the black band at the base of the beak. Blend back around the eye.

Load the dabber with Moon Yellow and add a touch at the bottom of the belly, working up toward the breast.

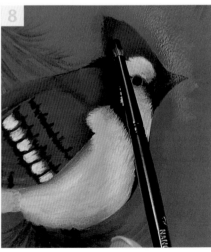

8 Dampen the head area with gel retarder. With Prussian Blue on the dabber, chisel shading into the upper beak and work back, chiseling into the blue area above the eye. Wipe the brush and lightly blend. Chisel a small amount of Prussian Blue into the back of the crest. Blend toward the beak. Let dry.

9 Make sure the white areas are dry and then redampen them with gel. Load the floral with Light Buttermilk. Begin in the middle of the breast and lighten toward the rump. Be sure you chisel over the wing at the shoulder. Wipe the brush and blend lightly. Chisel the light value on the white eyebrow into the blue crest and on the white throat area into the black neckband. Wipe the brush and blend away from the chiseling. You may also want to lighten the rump a bit, next to the tail.

10 Dampen the blue areas with gel. Load the dabber with a brush mix of Baby Blue + Victorian Blue. Lighten the middle of the crest. Wipe the brush and blend forward and backward. Lighten the middle of the back. Wipe the brush and blend. Lighten the shoulder of the foreground wing and pat to blend. Using the same brush mix, switch to a no. 1 liner and lighten between the two black wing bars. Lighten the top of the beak with Mix 1 on the dabber.

With a no. 12 flat, apply a light wash of Dioxazine Purple on the back to indicate wing separation. Apply the same wash at the back of the crest, working forward. Let the bird dry and then redampen with gel. Referring to the completed bird on page 98, build the lights with Light Buttermilk and the darks with Prussian Blue.

11 Using a no. 1 liner, paint the upper and lower eye-ring with Mix 2. Under the bottom eye-ring, outline with Mix 1. Under the Mix 1 outline, chisel in a slightly wider Light Buttermilk eye-ring. Under the Light Buttermilk, chisel in an eye-ring of Mix 1. Flatten the liner in Animal Black and side load with a bit of Mix 2. Paint a tiny C-shaped stroke outlining the pupil from 7 o'clock to 11 o'clock. Place a Light Buttermilk sparkle at 2 o'clock.

Flatten the no. 1 liner in Animal Black and side load with Mix 2. With Mix 2 facing right, paint along the right edge of the toes. Paint the claws in Animal Black. (Refer to the completed bird on page 98.) Let the painting dry completely and then varnish according to the directions on page 9.

YELLOW WARBLER

Sunshine and yellow warblers—now that's a perfect match. I look forward each spring to seeing these "balls of sunshine" darting through the trees. One recent spring, while I was painting in my studio, a pecking sound startled me. I looked to see a yellow warbler perched on top of my window feeder, pecking at his reflection. He either thought he was courting another warbler or was simply magnetized by his own beauty. Morning after morning, as I painted, he pecked. He finally left after about a month. I missed him and was glad I'd taken lots of photos.

Bird Materials

Paint: Acrylic, DecoArt Americana

Light Buttermilk

Moon Yellow

True Ochre

Cadmium Yellow

Raw Sienna

Burnt Sienna

Burnt Umber

Deep Burgundy

Animal Black:
Burnt Umber +
Lamp Black (2:1)

Mix 1: Light
Buttermilk +
Animal Black (2:1)

Mix 2: Light
Buttermilk +
Animal Black (3:1)

Surface
• 11" x 14" (27.9cm x 35.6cm) acid-free mounting board

Brushes
Loew-Cornell
• no. 8 flat
• no. 1 liner

Nancy Kinney Specialty
• small dabber
• floral

Other
• old scruffy brush for gel retarder
• 2-inch (51mm) wash for varnishing

Additional Supplies
• Jo Sonja's Gel Retarder   • paper towels for wiping brush
• J. W. etc.'s Right-Step Water Base Clear Varnish (Satin)

This pattern may be hand-traced or photocopied for personal use only. Enlarge at 243 percent to bring up to full size.

Background Materials

Paint: Acrylic, DecoArt Americana

Background: Arbor Green, True Ochre

Branch, leaves and cherries: Fawn, Animal Black (See bird colors.), Burnt Umber, Black Green, Deep Burgundy, True Red, Cadmium Orange, Antique Green, Celery Green

Brushes

- 2- to 4-inch (51mm to 102mm) sponge roller for basecoating
- 1-inch (25mm) wash
- no. 8 flat
- no. 1 liner
- dabber
- old scruffy

Additional Supplies

- 1-inch (25mm) diameter candle with holder
- old stainless steel tablespoon
- Krylon Matte Finish spray 1311
- gel retarder

1 Paint the background of your choice as described in chapter 3. I used a birch branch with green leaves, cherries and curlicues (see page 15) on a smoked surface with rouged color. Transfer the bird pattern.

Most bird basecoating can be done with a no. 8 flat, but if you have trouble in the smaller areas, change to a smaller flat or liner. Chisel the adjoining feather areas into each other as you go (see page 10 for explanation of chiseling). Apply your basecoat colors in this order: Animal Black on the outer tail edges; Cadmium Yellow on the inner tail feathers, the body and the head; Raw Sienna on the right wing; Mix 1 on the left wing and the beak; Animal Black on the eye and claws; Raw Sienna on the toes. Dampen the beak with gel retarder and separate the beak halves by adding a light value to the top half with Mix 2 and a touch of Mix 1 to the bottom half.

2 Let the bird dry. Then dip an old scruffy brush into the gel retarder. Wipe the excess on a paper towel and dampen the tail and wings. With Raw Sienna on the dabber, shade the upper tail, chiseling into the rump and working down the tail to separate the two tail sections.

With Burnt Umber on the dabber, shade the upper wing, chiseling into the yellow shoulder and working down the wing's left edge.

3 Side load Cadmium Yellow on the floral and paint small C-stokes to represent the feathers over the covert. Flat surface double load the floral with Burnt Sienna and Cadmium Yellow. With Cadmium Yellow facing the belly of the bird, paint the elongated C-stroke wing feather separations.

4 Dampen the head and body with gel. For most of this step you will be shading with Raw Sienna on the dabber. Always wipe the brush on a paper towel before blending. Shade the head by chiseling into the beak and extending the color around the eye. Blend into the head. Then shade the throat by chiseling into the beak. Blend down the throat. Shade under the wing and blend upward and downward. A Raw Sienna shadow is painted just above and below the branch. Blend the shading above the branch upward and below the branch downward. Slide shading on the back of the head and down the neck.

Now load your floral with Raw Sienna and use the chisel edge to create tiny Vs on the breast and belly for feather markings. Let dry.

5 Redampen the entire bird with gel. Reinforce all the shading in the previous step with Burnt Sienna. Be sure to add Burnt Sienna in the tiny Vs on the belly and breast. Let dry.

6 Redampen the bird with gel . Then load the tip of the floral in Deep Burgundy and apply a bit of color inside the points of the V-shaped feather markings on the breast and belly. Then apply Deep Burgundy down the back of the neck. Let dry.

7 Using the floral brush, apply a wash of Burnt Umber over all the Burnt Sienna shaded areas. Let dry.

Redampen the bird with gel. Enforce the light value on the top half of the beak with Mix 2 on the floral. Lighten the top of the head with a brush mix of Cadmium Yellow + Moon Yellow on the floral. Wipe the brush and blend toward the beak and down the back of the head. With the same brush and mix, lighten the cheek, the shoulder and into the breast, working as much as you can between the V-shaped feather markings. Wipe the brush and blend. Let dry.

8 Redampen with gel and further build the lights and darks as necessary. Paint the eye and feet details with a no. 1 liner. Use Moon Yellow for the eye-ring. Add a Light Buttermilk sparkle at 12 o'clock. Load the liner in True Ochre, side load with Burnt Umber and paint C-strokes along the toes with True Ochre placed on the left of each toe.

Let the painting dry completely and then varnish according to the directions on page 9.

ELEGANT TROGAN

I've never seen an elegant trogan, but other birders have told of their mystery and magnificence and have delighted me with photos.

The trogan lives in the canyons and on the desert floor of Arizona. They nest mostly in sycamore cavities near streams and only raise one brood per season. Some authorities think this is the main reason they are rare. Some feel they're growing extinct.

Native Americans believe the elegant trogan is possessed of the "blessing of the gods." The beauty of this bird does strongly indicate a one-of-a-kind blessing.

Bird Materials

Paint: Acrylic, DecoArt Americana

 Light Buttermilk

 Moon Yellow

 Cadmium Yellow

Burnt Sienna

True Red

Deep Burgundy

Prussian Blue

Black Plum

Black Forest Green

 Animal Black: Burnt Umber + Lamp Black (2:1)

 Mix 1: Light Buttermilk + Animal Black (2:1)

 Mix 2: Light Buttermilk + Animal Black (3:1)

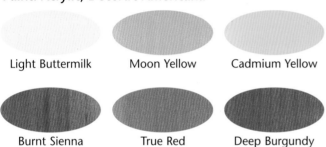

Surface
- 11" x 14" (27.9cm x 35.6cm) acid-free mounting board

Brushes
Loew-Cornell
- nos. 4 & 8 flats
- no. 1 liner

Nancy Kinney Specialty
- small dabber
- floral

Other
- old scruffy brush for gel retarder
- 2-inch (51mm) wash for varnishing

Additional Supplies
- Jo Sonja's Gel Retarder
- paper towels for wiping brush
- J. W. etc.'s Right-Step Water Base Clear Varnish (Satin)

This pattern may be hand-traced or photocopied for personal use only. Enlarge at 200 percent to bring up to full size.

Background Materials

Paint: Acrylic, DecoArt Americana

Background: Cashmere Beige, Black Green

Branch: Burnt Umber, Light Buttermilk

Brushes
- 2- to 4-inch (51mm to 102mm) sponge roller for basecoating
- 1-inch (25mm) wash
- no. 1 liner
- no. 8 flat
- old scruffy

Additional Supplies
- gel retarder

1 Paint the background of your choice as described in chapter 3. I used a twiggy branch on a blended-color surface. Transfer the bird pattern.

Most bird basecoating can be done with a no. 8 flat, but if you have trouble in the smaller areas, change to a smaller flat or liner. Chisel the adjoining feather areas into each other as you go (see page 10 for explanation of chiseling). Apply your basecoat colors in this order: Animal Black in the V between the tail feathers; Light Buttermilk on the white tail bars; Mix 2 on the remainder of the tail; Animal Black on the black tail bars (use a no. 1 liner); Mix 2 on the left wing; Mix 1 on the right wing; Deep Burgundy below the breast band and on the belly and rump; Light Buttermilk on the breast band; Black Forest Green on the head, neck and upper breast; Burnt Sienna on the eye; Cadmium Yellow on the beak; Animal Black on the feet. Let dry.

2 Dip an old scruffy brush into the gel retarder. Wipe the excess on a paper towel and dampen the tail. Using the dabber and Mix 1, chisel shading on the end of the tail. Wipe the brush and blend upward in a sweeping motion. While that area is still wet, apply and blend Animal Black in the same manner on the tips of the tail. On the tail, just below the rump, chisel Animal Black into the red rump. Wipe the brush and blend toward the black tail bars. Add Mix 1 shading between the black bars, chiseling into them. Wipe the brush and blend downward. Reinforce the black bars if necessary. Let dry.

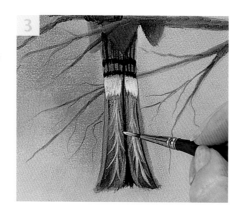

3 Redampen the tail with gel. Flatten the no. 1 liner in Animal Black and, using the chisel edge, indicate a few feather separations from the rump to the bottom of the black tail bar. Jump over the white tail bars and paint a few long tail feather separations in the bottom half of the tail. With the tail damp from the retarder, these feather lines should not be real strong. With Mix 2 on the liner, lighten the left and right outside tail edges and around the V-shaped shading at the end of the tail. Load the liner with Light Buttermilk and pull down the main feather vein in each half of the tail. Then add a few lines branching off as you would paint a tiny tree branch.

4 Dampen the wings with gel. On the left wing tip, shade near the branch with a small amount of Animal Black, using the dabber. Then shade the top of the right wing, chiseling into the green breast area. Wipe the brush and blend down the wing. With Light Buttermilk on the dabber, lighten the middle of the wing, wipe the brush and dab to blend. Let dry.

5 Redampen the right wing. Flat zsurface double load the floral with Mix 2 and Animal Black. With Mix 2 facing the breast of the bird, paint elongated C-stroke feather separations. Side load the floral with Mix 2 and paint small staggered C-strokes across the top of the wings, continuing with a few up the shoulder.

6 Dampen the breast band and the red areas with gel. Using Black Plum on the dabber, chisel shading on the red breast into the white breast band, under the wing, above the branch and below the branch. Wipe the brush and blend. Shade the white breast band with Mix 2, chiseling into the green area. Add Light Buttermilk to aid blending if needed. Wipe the brush and blend downward.

7 Dampen the head and neck with gel. Using Prussian Blue on the dabber, chisel shading into the beak and pull the color around the eye. Also shade under the beak and the cheek. Shade the beak with Burnt Sienna on a side-loaded no. 4 flat, blending toward the tip of the beak. With the chisel edge of the same brush, separate the top and bottom beak halves with Burnt Sienna. Let dry.

8 Dampen the red and white areas with gel. Using True Red on the dabber, lighten the middle of the belly. Wipe the brush and dab to blend, working the red up and down. You can further lighten with a brush mix of True Red + Cadmium Yellow. Lighten the breast band with Light Buttermilk on the chisel edge of the floral.

9 Dampen the head with gel. Wipe off the excess on a paper towel. Brush-mix Prussian Blue + Cadmium Yellow, and, using the chisel edge of the dabber, lighten the top of the head, the cheek, the middle of the breast and the area just above the top of the wing. Wipe the brush after each area and blend in the direction of feather growth. If necessary, add Prussian Blue for a softer blending.

Lighten the top of the beak with Moon Yellow on a no. 4 flat. Let the entire bird dry.

10 Redampen the bird with gel and further build the lights and darks as necessary. Paint the eye and feet details with a no. 1 liner. Paint the pupil Animal Black, leaving left and right edges of Burnt Sienna showing. Use Mix 2 for the eye-ring. Add a Light Buttermilk sparkle at 10 o'clock. Flatten the liner in Animal Black and side load with Mix 2. With Mix 2 facing left, paint along the left edge of the toes. Paint the claws Animal Black.

Let the painting dry completely and then varnish according to the directions on page 9.

RUBY-THROATED HUMMINGBIRD

I have to admit, one of the main reasons I love spring is that it's when I hang my hummingbird feeder on my studio window and watch for the first sipper. When I first tried to attract hummingbirds, I waited two years before the first hummer arrived. Now the feeder is only out a couple of days before they flutter up, seeking the sweet nectar.

I've found it's almost impossible to see the hummingbirds' tiny wings because of their constant darting. When they're in flight, their wings are a blur. To indicate this movement, I kept the wing detail minimal.

Bird Materials

Paint: Acrylic, DecoArt Americana

Light Buttermilk	Cadmium Yellow	True Ochre
True Red	Deep Burgundy	Black Plum
Prussian Blue	Black Forest Green	Grey Sky
Animal Black: Burnt Umber + Lamp Black (2:1)	Mix 1: Light Buttermilk + Animal Black (2:1)	Mix 2: Light Buttermilk + Animal Black (3:1)

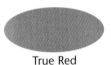

Surface
- wooden plate, 11½" x 11½" (29.2cm x 29.2cm) available from The Artist's Club (see Resources, page 126.)

Brushes
Loew-Cornell
- no. 8 flat
- no. 1 liner

Nancy Kinney Specialty
- small dabber
- floral

Other
- old scruffy brush for gel retarder
- 2-inch (51mm) wash for varnishing

Additional Supplies
- Jo Sonja's Gel Retarder
- paper towels for wiping brush
- J. W. etc.'s Right-Step Water Base Clear Varnish (Satin)

Background Materials

Paint: Acrylic, DecoArt Americana
Background: Arbor Green, Light Buttermilk

Daisy, stem, leaves with curlicues: Light Buttermilk, Deep Burgundy, Mix 1 (See bird colors.), Black Plum, Black Green, True Ochre, True Red, Cadmium Yellow, Hauser Medium Green, thinned Black Green (for curlicues)

Brushes
- 2- to 4-inch (51mm to 102mm) sponge roller for basecoating
- nos. 4 & 8 flats
- no. 1 liner
- small dabber
- old scruffy

Additional Supplies
- gel retarder

These patterns may be hand-traced or photocopied for personal use only
Enlarge at 200 percent to bring up to full size.

1 Paint the background of your choice as described in chapter 3. I used a daisy and leaves on a rolled surface. Transfer the bird pattern.

Most bird basecoating can be done with a no. 8 flat, but if you have trouble in the smaller areas, change to a smaller flat or liner. Chisel the adjoining feather areas into each other as you go (see page 10 for explanation of chiseling). Apply your basecoat colors in this order: Black Forest Green on the top of the head, at the base of the front wing and on the tail; Mix 2 on the back wing and the primaries of the foreground wing; Mix 1 on the front wing secondaries; Light Buttermilk on the neckband; Deep Burgundy on the throat; Grey Sky on the breast, belly and rump; Animal Black on the eye and the bottom beak half; Mix 2 on the top beak half; Mix 1 on the foot.

Let the bird dry. Then dip an old scruffy brush into the gel retarder. Wipe the excess on a paper towel and dampen the wings. Load the dabber with Animal Black and shade the back wing to separate it from the front wing. Also chisel this Animal Black shading under the front wing toward the gray body. Wipe the brush and blend toward the bird's back.

Side load the floral in Light Buttermilk and pull in a few hints of back wing-feather separations, starting at the wing tips and lifting the brush as you approach the bird's back. Load Light Buttermilk on the chisel edge of the floral and paint the top feather separation on the front wing.

2 Pick up a touch of Black Forest Green and work it into the secondary wing feathers on the front wing. Then paint a Black Forest Green wash over the entire back wing.

3 Double load the floral with Animal Black and Light Buttermilk and, with the Light Buttermilk facing the bird, pull in the remaining elongated feather separations. Start your strokes at the feather tips. Side load with Light Buttermilk and chisel in wing covert separations in small staggered C-shapes.

4 Dampen the green areas with the gel retarder. Wipe excess from the brush. With Prussian Blue on the dabber, shade the tail and back, chiseling into the rump and on up to the neck. Wipe the brush and blend toward the top of the bird. Chisel Prussian Blue on the face into the beak, into the red throat area and all around the eye. Wipe the brush and blend into the head.

5 With Mix 2 on the dabber, shade the white neck ring where it meets the red throat, chiseling into this red area. Wipe the brush and blend down the neck. With Black Plum on the dabber, shade the red throat, chiseling into the green head. Wipe the brush and blend down into the red area. Then paint staggered C-strokes in the red throat area with Black Plum.

6 Dampen the gray area with gel. Using a no. 8 flat, add a thin layer of Grey Sky to aid in blending. Using Light Buttermilk on the floral, chisel this light value into the rump. Work on up into the belly, picking up a bit of True Ochre. Wipe the brush and blend toward the tail. Load the brush in Light Buttermilk and stagger short chiseling strokes up the body to indicate feather markings. Then chisel Light Buttermilk over the green wing-and-body separation. Wipe the brush and blend back into the gray area.

7 Make sure the head and throat are dry and then redampen them with gel. Brush-mix Prussian Blue + Cadmium Yellow on the floral and lighten the middle of the green portion of the head. Wipe the brush and blend forward and backward. Load True Red on the floral and chisel inside the Black Plum C-shaped strokes on the throat. Further lighten the top half of the beak with the chisel edge of the floral with Light Buttermilk.

8 Let the bird dry and then redampen with gel. Further build the lights and darks as necessary. Use Cadmium Yellow on the top of the head and Light Buttermilk on the chiseled strokes on the breast and belly.

Paint the eye and feet details with a no. 1 liner. Use Mix 2 for the eye-ring, but notice that the ring doesn't go completely around the eye. Instead paint C-strokes at the front and the back of the eye. Flatten the liner in Animal Black and side load with a bit of Mix 2. Paint a thin C-stroke from 7 o'clock to 5 o'clock to mark the outside of the pupil edge. Add a Light Buttermilk sparkle at 2 o'clock.

Let the painting dry completely and then varnish according to the directions on page 9.

ROSE-BREASTED GROSBEAK

What was that mystery bird that just flew by? It's rare to see a rose-breasted grosbeak in the South, where I live, but while teaching in the Toronto area, I was lucky enough to get a glimpse of this bird sitting on a limb when I stepped outside for a breath of air. He quickly grabbed a dried berry and departed, for I had startled him. If only he'd known how much I just wanted to gaze upon his beauty!

The rose-breasted grosbeak lives in the woods along streams, and his nest, built high in the trees, is a flimsy-looking shallow cup of twigs.

Bird Materials

Paint: Acrylic, DecoArt Americana

Light Buttermilk

French Vanilla

Black Forest Green

True Red

Deep Burgundy

Burnt Sienna

Black Plum

Animal Black: Burnt Umber + Lamp Black (2:1)

Mix 1: Light Buttermilk + Animal Black (2:1)

Mix 2: Light Buttermilk + Animal Black (3:1)

Surface
• 11" x 14" (27.9cm x 35.6cm) acid-free mounting board

Brushes
Loew-Cornell
• nos. 4 & 8 flats
• no. 1 liner

Nancy Kinney Specialty
• small dabber
• floral

Other
• old scruffy brush for gel retarder
• 2-inch (51mm) wash for varnishing

Additional Supplies
• Jo Sonja's Gel Retarder
• J. W. etc.'s Right-Step Water Base Clear Varnish (Satin)
• paper towels for wiping brush

This pattern may be hand-traced or photocopied for personal use only. Enlarge at 200 percent to bring up to full size.

Background Materials

Paint: Acrylic, DecoArt Americana

Background: Arbor Green, Black Forest Green, Deep Burgundy

Branch: Fawn, Burnt Umber

Brushes

- 2- to 4-inch (51mm to 102mm) sponge roller for basecoating
- no. 8 flat
- old scruffy
- no. 1 liner

Additional Supplies

- plastic wrap
- spray mist water bottle
- large sea sponge
- gel retarder

1 Paint the background of your choice as described in chapter 3. I used a twiggy branch on a sponge-and-plastic wrap surface treatment. Transfer the bird pattern.

Most bird basecoating can be done with a no. 8 flat, but if you have trouble in the smaller areas, change to a smaller flat or liner. Chisel the adjoining feather areas into each other as you go (see page 10 for explanation of chiseling). Apply your basecoat colors in this order: Light Buttermilk on the middle tail feathers; Animal Black on the outer tail feathers, the wing, head, eye and feet; French Vanilla on the beak, adding a tiny V of Animal Black to the tip of the beak top. Light Buttermilk on the belly, rump and wing bar; Deep Burgundy on the breast.

2 Let the bird dry. Then dip an old scruffy brush into the gel retarder. Wipe the excess on a paper towel and dampen the white areas. Use the dabber and Mix 1 to shade the tail as it goes under the covert. Chisel into the covert and then wipe the brush and blend toward the tail. Shade the covert, chiseling into the rump. Wipe the brush and blend toward the covert tip.

Still using the dabber, shade the outer edge of the belly, chiseling toward the red breast. Wipe the brush and pick up a tiny bit of Black Forest Green to chisel right over the breast. This will create a color reflection from the surrounding foliage. Shade with Mix 1 at the top of the larger white portion of the breast, chiseling into the red portion of the breast. Wipe the brush and blend toward the belly and along the bottom of the body. Again, pick up a tiny amount of Black Forest Green to chisel over the Mix 1 along the bottom of the body.

Shade the upper areas of the wing bar with Mix 1 on the dabber. Wipe the brush and pull lightly down on the chisel edge to create bar-feather separations.

3 Dampen all the black areas with gel. Use the chisel edge of the floral to separate the black tail feathers with Mix 2. Then paint the wing-feather separations in elongated C-strokes, starting near the wing bar. Load the no. 1 liner with Light Buttermilk to paint short comma-like stroke separations between the long ones. Then load the liner in Animal Black and further separate the wing-bar feathers.

4 While the black areas remain damp, load Mix 2 on the dabber to add the light value to the head and shoulder. Always wipe the brush before blending, and add Animal Black if the light value does not blend softly. Start by adding Mix 2 to the top of the shoulder, blending the lower edge. Next lighten the forehead, blending forward and backward. Next comes the cheek, which is blended to the left and right. Next lighten from the beak corner downward and soften. Then lighten under the neck, blending up and down.

5 Side load a no. 4 flat with Burnt Sienna. Paint where the beak is attached to the head. Wipe the brush and chisel slightly back toward the head and out toward the tip of the beak. Pick up a tiny bit of Burnt Sienna and shade the bottom beak tip, working back. Separate the upper and lower beak halves with Animal Black on the no. 1 liner.

6 Load the dabber with Black Plum and shade under the black neckband and on the left side of the red breast, chiseling into the black neckband and into the white breast and belly on the left. Wipe the brush and blend.

With True Red on the floral, lighten the right side of the red breast, chiseling over the white breast area on the right.

7 Further build the lights and darks as necessary. Paint the eye and feet details with a no. 1 liner. Use Mix 2 for the eye-ring. Then with a C-stroke from 3 o'clock to 5 o'clock, lighten the pupil outline. Add a Light Buttermilk sparkle at 10 o'clock. Flatten the liner in Animal Black and side load with Mix 2. With Mix 2 facing left, paint along the left edge of the toes. Paint the claws Animal Black.

Let the painting dry completely and then varnish according to the directions on page 9.

What a creation! I enjoyed bringing this bird to life in my painting.

Waxwings in general look very much alike, including the European waxwings. They're known for their unusual coloring and prominent crest.

The Bohemian Waxwing, like all waxwings, lives where berry-bearing trees are found, including hedgerows, parks and gardens. They'll wander throughout their native country in search of a good fruit crop.

Bird Materials

Paint: Acrylic, DecoArt Americana

Light Buttermilk

Cadmium Yellow

Moon Yellow

True Ochre

Raw Sienna

Burnt Sienna

Burnt Umber

True Red

Animal Black:
Burnt Umber +
Lamp Black (2:1)

Mix 1: Light
Buttermilk +
Animal Black (2:1)

Mix 2: Light
Buttermilk +
Animal Black (3:1)

Surface
• 11" x 14" (27.9cm x 35.6cm) acid-free mounting board

Brushes

Loew-Cornell
• nos. 4 & 8 flats
• no. 1 liner

Nancy Kinney Specialty
• small dabber
• floral

Other
• old scruffy brush for gel retarder
• 2-inch (51mm) wash for varnishing

Additional Supplies
• Jo Sonja's Gel Retarder   • paper towels for wiping brush
• J. W. etc.'s Right-Step Water Base Clear Varnish (Satin)

This pattern may be hand-traced or photocopied for personal use only. Enlarge at 200 percent to bring up to full size.

Background Materials

Paint: Acrylic, DecoArt Americana

Background: Driftwood

Branch, leaves and cherries: Burnt Umber, Light Buttermilk, Animal Black (See bird colors.), Antique Green, Black Green, Celery Green, Deep Burgundy

Brushes
- 2- to 4-inch (51mm to 102mm) sponge roller for basecoating
- no. 8 flat
- no. 1 liner
- small dabber
- old scruffy

Additional Supplies
- gel retarder

1 Paint the background of your choice as described in chapter 3. I used a branch with green leaves, cherries and curlicues on a rolled surface.

Transfer the bird pattern.

Most bird basecoating can be done with a no. 8 flat, but if you have trouble in the smaller areas, change to a smaller flat or liner. Chisel the adjoining feather areas into each other as you go (see page 10 for explanation of chiseling). Apply your basecoat colors in this order: Cadmium Yellow on the tail tips; Animal Black on the remaining tail and the wings; Burnt Umber on the coverts; Animal Black on the mask and under the neck; Light Buttermilk for white wing and neck details; True Red for wing details; Mix 1 on the beak; Animal Black on the eye and feet; Raw Sienna on the crown and remainder of the body. Let dry.

2 Dip an old scruffy brush into the gel retarder. Wipe the excess on a paper towel and dampen the tail, wings and covert. Using the dabber, work Mix 2 into the tail and foreground wing to slightly lighten. Wipe the brush and pat to blend.

Flat surface double load the floral with Animal Black and Mix 2. Using the chisel edge with Mix 2 facing the belly, pull in tail feather separations in elongated C-strokes. Paint feather edges on the wings in the same manner. Using the floral brush and Animal Black, paint separations on the yellow tail tips.

Using Animal Black, paint a shadow line to separate the coverts. This will be painted on the shoulder of the back covert. Then chisel the Animal Black shadow into the Raw Sienna at the breast and neck. Wipe the brush and blend toward the wing.

3 Dampen the body and head with gel. Using Animal Black on the dabber, chisel shading on top of the head into the mask. Then add a small amount of shading on the back of the crest. Wipe the brush and blend both shadings toward the middle of the head. Now chisel shading into the underside of the white face and neck detail, working toward the back of the head and then under the neck. Shade down the outside edge of the body front, behind the leaf and under the wing. Wipe the brush and blend.

With a no. 4 flat, side load with Animal Black and paint a shadow where the beak is attached to the head. Wipe the brush and blend toward the beak tip. Separate the top and bottom beak halves with a line of Animal Black. Let dry.

4 Redampen the body and head with gel. Using the dabber, apply a thin coat of Raw Sienna to the unshaded Raw Sienna undercoat. At this point you will be working with a wet-on-wet technique.

Using True Ochre on the floral, lighten the crown and crest. Wipe the brush and blend forward and backward. Chisel True Ochre on the shoulder into the top of the coverts. Also apply True Ochre on the side of the wing and down the breast and belly. Wipe the brush and add a bit of Burnt Sienna under the wing, above the rump, in the V of the white face detail and above the eye area in the crown. Let dry.

5 Redampen the bird with gel. Further build lights on the crown, above the covert and in the belly with Moon Yellow using the floral. Lighten the top half of the beak with Mix 2 on the chisel edge of the floral. Let dry.

6 Redampen the bird with gel and further build the lights and darks as necessary. Paint the eye and feet and white neck and facial details with a no. 1 liner. Use Mix 2 for the top of the eye-ring. Add a Light Buttermilk sparkle at 11 o'clock. There is a white band just below the eye. Using the liner, add a tiny amount of Mix 1 just under the eye, blending down into this white eye band. To paint the feet, flatten the liner in Animal Black and side load with Mix 2. With Animal Black on the left edge, paint a series of tiny C-strokes across the toes. Tone down all the white feather details with a wash of Animal Black.

Let the painting dry completely and then varnish according to the directions on page 9.

When God created the painted bunting, He must have been in a really cheerful mood. No other bird in North America is more colorful.

Despite their amazing colors, painted buntings aren't easy to find. They blend into their surroundings surprisingly well by staying in thick cover. The early spring mating season provides the best chance of spotting the colorful males. They're quite the singers, which makes them easier to locate as they perch in sunny spots, hoping to attract a mate.

Bird Materials

Paint: Acrylic, DecoArt Americana

Light Buttermilk	Cadmium Yellow	True Red

Deep Burgundy	Black Plum	Baby Blue

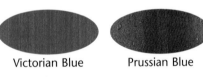

Victorian Blue	Prussian Blue	Hauser Medium Green

Black Green	Animal Black: Burnt Umber + Lamp Black (2:1)	Mix 2: Light Buttermilk + Animal Black (3:1)

Surface
• 11" x 14" (27.9cm x 35.6cm) acid-free mounting board

Brushes
Loew-Cornell
• nos. 4 & 8 flats
• no. 1 liner

Nancy Kinney Specialty
• small dabber
• floral

Other
• old scruffy brush for gel retarder
• 2-inch (51mm) wash for varnishing

Additional Supplies
• Jo Sonja's Gel Retarder   • paper towels for wiping brush
• J. W. etc.'s Right-Step Water Base Clear Varnish (Satin)

This pattern may be hand-traced or photocopied for personal use only. Enlarge at 200 percent to bring up to full size.

Background Materials

Paint: Acrylic, DecoArt Americana

Background: Grey Sky

Branches, leaves and curlicues: Animal Black (See bird colors.), Light Buttermilk, Hauser Medium Green, Black Green, Cadmium Yellow

Brushes

- 2- to 4-inch (51mm to 102mm) sponge roller for basecoating
- no. 8 flat
- small dabber
- no. 1 liner
- old scruffy

Additional Supplies

- gel retarder

1 Paint the background of your choice as described in chapter 3. I used a branch with green leaves (holly) on a rolled surface. Later I added curlicues. Transfer the bird pattern.

Most bird basecoating can be done with a no. 8 flat, but if you have trouble in the smaller areas, change to a smaller flat or liner. Chisel the adjoining feather areas into each other as you go (see page 10 for explanation of chiseling). Apply your basecoat colors in this order: Animal Black on the tail, wing, feet, beak and eye; Deep Burgundy on the tail covert, rump, belly, breast and throat; Hauser Medium Green on the wing covert; Victorian Blue on the head.

2 Let the bird dry. Then dip an old scruffy brush into the gel retarder, wipe the excess on a paper towel and dampen the tail, wing and the green wing covert. Using Black Green on the dabber, shade the green covert, chiseling into the head and the red area. Wipe the brush and blend down the wing. To separate the green wing bar from the covert, chisel in a short bar of Black Green.

PAINTED BUNTING, continued

3 Dampen the red area with gel. Using the dabber and Black Plum, shade under the left edge of the bird from the neck to the rump and also under the wing. Wipe the brush and blend by stroking back and forth where the Black Plum meets the Deep Burgundy. To separate the rump area from the belly, dab in a little Black Plum in a chiseling motion.

4 Dampen the head with gel. Using Prussian Blue on the dabber, shade the face, chiseling into the beak and pulling the color around the eye, under the cheek and down the left edge of the blue hood, chiseling into the red throat area. Add a bit of shading to the back of the head and neck.

Lighten the top of the beak with Mix 2 on a no. 4 flat. Let the bird dry.

5 Dampen the wing with gel. Using the no. 1 liner and Animal Black, separate the green wing bars into five sections. Lighten the bottom tips of these sections with a brush mix of Cadmium Yellow + Hauser Medium Green, chiseling into the lower wing. Flat surface double load the floral with Animal Black and Hauser Medium Green. With the Hauser Medium Green facing left, paint tail and wing feather separations. You can see the entire tail with its feather separations in the next photo. Let dry.

6 Dampen the green wing covert and the red areas of the bird. Lighten the wing covert with a brush mix of Hauser Medium Green + Cadmium Yellow on the dabber. Chisel this color over the black wing edge. Wipe the brush and blend upward.

Using True Red on the floral, lighten the rump, chiseling over the tail. Wipe the brush and blend upward. Then lighten the belly and breast area, chiseling over the blue and green areas. Wipe the brush and blend.

7 Using Baby Blue on the floral, lighten the top of the head. Wipe the brush and blend toward the front and the back of the head. Apply Baby Blue on the cheek area. Wipe the brush and blend slightly up toward the eye. Apply the same light value on the shoulder, chiseling over the green covert. Wipe the brush and blend upward. Let the entire bird dry.

8 Redampen the entire bird with gel. With the floral, further lighten the wing covert with Cadmium Yellow and the red areas with a brush mix of True Red + Cadmium Yellow. Reinforce the head shadows with Prussian Blue and further lighten with Baby Blue. Lighten the top of the beak with Light Buttermilk on a no. 4 flat. Add a tiny amount of Victorian Blue on the top and the bottom of the beak.

Paint the eye and feet details with a no. 1 liner. Use Deep Burgundy for the eye-ring. Flatten the liner in Animal Black and side load with Mix 2. Paint a tiny C-stroke in the left and the right corners of the pupil. Add a Light Buttermilk sparkle at 10 o'clock. Flatten the liner in Animal Black and side load with Mix 2. With Mix 2 facing left, paint along the left edge of the toes. Paint the claws with Animal Black, using the liner.

Let the painting dry completely and then varnish according to the directions on page 9.

Resources

Brushes

Nancy Kinney's Paintin' House
  for floral and dabber brushes
421 14th Avenue NW
Hickory, North Carolina 28601
Phone: 828-327-2478
E:mail: kinney@twave.net
www.PictureTrail.com/nancykinney

Loew-Cornell, Inc.
563 Chestnut Avenue.,
Teaneck, NJ 07666
Phone: 201-836-7070
E-mail: loew-cornell@loew-cornell.com
www.loew-cornell.com

Paints and Mediums

Chroma Inc. USA
  for Jo Sonja's Gel Retarder
205 Bucky Drive
Lititz, PA 17543
Phone: 800-257-8278
Fax: 717-626-9292
www.chromaonline.com

DecoArt
P.O. Box 386
Stanford, KY 40484
Phone: 800-367-3047
www.decoart.com

J.W. etc. Quality Products
  for varnish
2205 First Street, Suite 103
Simi Valley, CA 93065
www.jwetc.com

Nancy Kinney's Paintin' House
  for Animal Black acrylic
See contact information under Brushes.

Surfaces and Mats

The Artist's Club
  for wooden plates
13118 NE 4th Street
Vancouver, WA 98684
Phone: 800-845-6507
www.artistsclub.com

Masterson Art Products, Inc.
  for Sta-Wet Palettes
P.O. Box 11301
Phoenix, AZ 85017
Phone: 800-965-2675
www.mastersonart.com

Nancy Kinney's Paintin' House
  for painting surfaces and mats
See contact information under Brushes.

Canadian Retailers

Crafts Canada
2745 29th Street Northeast
Calgary, AL, T1Y 7B5

Folk Art Enterprises
P.O. Box 1088
Ridgetown, ON, N0P 2C0
Tel: 888-214-0062

MacPherson Craft Wholesale
83 Queen Street East
P.O. Box 1870
St. Mary's, ON, N4X 1C2
Tel: 519-284-1741

Maureen McNaughton Enterprises Inc.
Rural Route #2
Belwood, ON, N0B 1J0
Tel: 519-843-5648
Fax: 519-843-6022
E-mail: maureen.mcnaughton.ent.inc
@sympatico.ca
www.maureenmcnaughton.com

Mercury Art & Craft Supershop
332 Wellington Street
London, ON, N6C 4P7
Tel: 519-434-1636

Town & Country Folk Art Supplies
93 Green Lane
Thornhill, ON, L3T 6K6
Tel: 905-882-0199

U.K. Retailers

Art Express
Design House
Sizers Court
Yeadon LS19 6DP
Tel: 0113 250 0077
www.artexpress.co.uk

Atlantis Art Materials
146 Brick Lane
London E1 6RU
Tel: 020 7377 8855

Crafts World (head office)
No. 8 North Street, Guildford
Surrey GU1 4AF
Tel: 07000 757070

Green & Stone
259 King's Road
London SW3 5EL
Tel: 020 7352 0837
E-mail: greenandstone@enterprise.net

Hobby Crafts (head office)
River Court
Southern Sector
Bournemouth International Airport
Christchurch
Dorset BH23 6SE
Tel: 0800 272387

Homecrafts Direct
P.O. Box 38
Leicester LE1 9BU
Tel: 0116 251 3139

INDEX

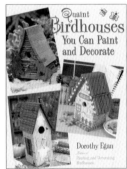

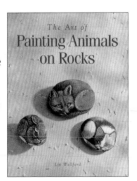